COMING OF AGE AT THE
Focal Point

HOW SENIOR CENTERS ENHANCE
QUALITY OF LIFE FOR OLDER ADULTS

ALTHIA ELLIS

COMING OF AGE AT THE
Focal Point

HOW SENIOR CENTERS ENHANCE
QUALITY OF LIFE FOR OLDER ADULTS

ALTHIA ELLIS

TATE PUBLISHING
AND ENTERPRISES, LLC

Published by Tate Publishing & Enterprises, LLC
127 E. Trade Center Terrace | Mustang, Oklahoma 73064 USA
1.888.361.9473 | www.tatepublishing.com

Tate Publishing is committed to excellence in the publishing industry. The company reflects the philosophy established by the founders, based on Psalm 68:11,
"The Lord gave the word and great was the company of those who published it."

Book design copyright © 2013 by Tate Publishing, LLC. All rights reserved.
Cover design by Joel Uber
Interior design by Caypeeline Casas
Artistic Illustrations by Dajon Gordon

Published in the United States of America

ISBN: 978-1-62510-344-4
1. Social Science / Gerontology
2. Family & Relationships / Eldercare
13.09.05

Dedication

This book is dedicated to my beautiful parents,
Robert and Norma; and to my son,
Tariq and daughter, Oriana.

Acknowledgments

This book is dedicated to my parents, Robert and Norma Thompson, two beautiful, caring and spiritual individuals whom I adore and will forever love, admire, and emulate. You have cultivated in me a spirit of love, compassion, good will and an appreciation for all people. You have always been so caring and skilled at managing your resources and it puzzled me, even as a child, how you could have been so generous to so many people throughout your lives and even today. It is very clear to me now. You have figured out that a life of love, friendship, integrity, simplicity, and yes, challenges unending, can be worthwhile and fulfilling. Thank you for being my heroes. Thank you for believing in me and for always encouraging me to aim high and be the best that I can be. This one is for you, Mom and Dad, with love and admiration always!

And, thank you to my two precious children, Oriana and Tariq. You are my pride and joy; you put a smile on my face always. To my dear husband and friend, Rohan, thank you for being the protector of our family and for always dishing up great advice—you're the best!

Finally, I give praise to the Almighty for His direction and endless blessings.

Table of Contents

Preface 11

PART I

Starting the Journey............................ 17

A New Challenge 25

The Principals 31

What's In a Senior Center? 39

Older Adults as Volunteers 45

Seniors at Play................................ 57

The Mobility Factor........................... 75

Healthy Choices 93

Staying Put 115

Paying Respect................................ 125

PART II

It's Not the End of the Journey 133

Epilogue 149
Appendix A 153
Appendix B................................ 169

Preface

The accounts in this book are based primarily on my observation of and interaction with older adults who attended a senior center where I worked and served for fourteen years. They laughed, they played, they experienced good and bad days, they shared with each other and reminisced often, and it was very clear that most tried desperately to maintain their independence and dignity. This meant much to them. As I observed their behaviors from a distance and interacted with them from time to time, I could not help but wonder what it will be like when my parents arrive at that stage of their lives. I would like for them to be able to laugh, have fun, be active, enjoy life, and not be too concerned about the mundane things of this world. I wonder, too, what it will be like when I get to that stage of my life. Perhaps the journey that I went on when I wrote this book will help me plan that chapter.

I have found that there is a basic lack of understanding about what a senior center is and does, who can receive services, and what types of services are available. Some seniors are just not sure how they would fit in at a senior center and more importantly, how beneficial participation in the programs might be to them. This book will help to clarify any doubts or misunderstandings.

I like to describe senior centers as playgrounds for older adults. They show up whenever they wish, volunteer as they like, have fun with whomever they choose, participate in special programs as much or as little as they want, and leave when they have had enough. Typically the faces you will see at senior centers are those of individuals who are upwards of fifty years old.

Many older adults regard senior centers as their sanctuary. It is a place where they can access programs and services that in many ways impact their golden years. The opportunities are endless: a wide variety of indoor and outdoor activities, delicious and nutritious meals, intergenerational programs, education and healthcare programs, case management services, and so much more.

Thanks to the Older Americans Act (OAA) of 1965—a unique and highly regarded statute that has stimulated the development of a comprehensive and coordinated service system—older adults have more opportunities to help maintain their dignity and welfare. The OAA has greatly impacted the lives of older individuals, family caregivers, and persons with disabilities in the United States, and has become the primary source for organizing, coordinating, and providing community-based services, such as senior centers and opportunities for older Americans and their families.

With the baby-boom population approaching old age, one wonders how the rapidly increasing numbers and diverse lifestyles of these boomers will impact the image of today's senior centers. While center administrators are struggling with redefining the senior center image, many older adults are taking advantage of this dynamic community resource. I realize that senior centers must compete with other organizations offering similar services to older adults, but they still hold a coveted position in meeting the needs of the elderly. Today, close to 11,000 senior centers nationwide bring joy to almost a million older adults daily. The table below shows the categories of generations by age.

GENERATIONS	YEARS OF BIRTH	AGES IN 2012
Gen Z	Born 1993-2004	Ages 8-19
Millennials	Born 1977-1993	Ages 18-34
Gen X	Born 1965-1976	Ages 34-46
Younger Boomers	Born 1955-1964	Ages 47-56
Older Boomers	Born 1946-1954	Ages 57-65
Silent Generation	Born 1937-1945	Ages 66-74
G.I. Generation	Born before 1936	Ages 76 and older

I am very excited about sharing my senior center experiences with you. The images are fascinating; they expose a lifestyle that is worth sharing with people of all ages. After reading this book, it will be up to you to decide whether the resources offered at senior centers and other community centers across the nation can indeed benefit you, a family member, a neighbor, or a friend. Additionally, having been exposed to the purpose that senior centers serve, I sincerely hope that each person will play a role in helping to revive a culture of respect and honor for older people.

PART I

Starting the Journey

It was a beautiful, Florida morning when I pulled into the oddly-shaped parking lot of the senior center. I was there for an interview. I pulled in my car slowly and circled the lot, searching for a parking space as I eyeballed the facility.

It was an old, single-story, off-white building. I was unaware of the history that surrounded it. It did not take me very long to find a parking space and I carefully settled in.

As I attempted to check my make-up in the mirror, something immediately caught my attention. It was a black and white sign, which read, "Day Care."

I gasped. "Day Care," I whispered to myself.

My heart began pounding rapidly. Were my eyes deceiving me? Could it be what I was thinking—a children's Day Care program?

It couldn't be! This would be the perfect arrangement, thinking now of my young daughter. How convenient it would be for me to have my daughter at a day care center just a stone's throw away from my place of employment!

Almost immediately I had to perish the thought as my mind reverted to the purpose of my visit. I stepped from the vehicle cautiously. I must admit that I was a bit nervous because this was my first job interview in five years. Car doors closed and locked and I gingerly made my way toward the main entrance of the building, all the while walking as if all eyes were upon me.

I entered the lobby with an ample sense of control and confidence and greeted the smiling receptionist. I promptly introduced myself, and announced my purpose for being there. The receptionist, an older Caucasian woman, was warm and helpful and directed me to an old chair to await my interviewers.

As I made myself comfortable on the worn sofa, I heard the receptionist announce my arrival on the telephone to someone whose name I did not recognize. As she hung up the receiver, she glanced in my direction and smiled warmly. I returned a quick smile. As I waited, my eyes started to scour the small and cozy lobby with its pictures, paintings, and other artwork hanging on the wall—some hanging slightly crooked.

I wondered what was behind the door next to the receptionist—classrooms and offices maybe. Next to the lobby, I noticed a large airy room in which sat several older adults, both men and women. Some were talking among themselves, some were reading the newspaper while having coffee, and others just milled around. Most of them seemed content. The expression on some of the faces of these people indicated that they wanted to be left alone. As I gazed into the large, airy room, two women got up from their chairs and started walking in my direction. The women chatted happily as they walked along. As they passed by me, they offered a friendly and generous greeting. I responded with an equally kind greeting and a warm smile. They surprised me.

After the women had passed, I turned my attention once again to the large room and noticed that a few more people were entering the room from different directions. I wondered what the plan of action was for these senior adults, and was curious about whether this was a daily routine for them. The answer came almost immediately. From the corner of one eye I could see what appeared to be an old magazine rack. I turned to see several magazines, a few books, and some newspapers sitting on the rack. I quickly glanced at the "mini library" and picked up an exercise magazine. It was outdated with torn pages. As I thumbed through the pages of the magazine I came upon what appeared to be a calendar. I took a closer look and realized that it was an activity schedule for the seniors. I opened the calendar to find listings of available services, upcoming events and happenings for seniors at the center, daily activities, as well as a listing of important phone numbers. At that moment, it occurred to me that the seniors in the large, airy room were just preparing themselves for the myriad of activities that the day held in store for them. By all appearances, the month of March seemed to be a busy one.

As I read the pages of the activity calendar, my mind reverted to the "Day Care" sign and I was tempted to discuss it with the kind receptionist. However, I quickly decided against it, concluding that I should instead be preparing for the interview while I waited. Only a few minutes later my interviewers appeared. I just knew it had to be them as soon as I saw the two women approaching from a narrow hallway. As they came closer, one of them called out my first name, and I quickly stood and spilled out a bright "Hello, good morning!" We shook hands. They were just as warm as the receptionist as they introduced themselves. After the greeting, they briskly escorted me down the narrow hallway. As I followed them, I managed to steal a few glances at the staff workstations and the equipment stacked against the wall along the hallway. There were employees busy at their workstations, which were very small.

At the end of the hallway, we entered a quaint, yet spacious, office where my interviewers offered me a chair. Almost immediately, the scent of fresh potpourri punctured the air in the room as I seated myself. As the two women got comfortable in their seats, I scanned the room quickly. Its age showed, and there were boxes in one corner and small piles of documents on the desktop as well as on the floor. A bookshelf in one corner supported stacks of magazines, books, and files. The sunlight danced through the vertical blinds covering the large windows and I looked outside and realized that my car was parked in the lot close to the office. For a few seconds, my eyes remained fixed on the window as I wondered whether the women had observed my arrival. Maybe they weren't even paying attention; maybe the blinds were still closed, I speculated.

I have been nervous at other interviews, but surprisingly, I felt fairly comfortable at this one. The lead interviewer thanked me again for coming and verified that I was there for the vacant part time Volunteer Services Coordinator position. She asked me to share a little about myself and soon, I was responding to a slew of questions. Both individuals took turns explaining the general programs and services, as well as the responsibilities and expectations of the position. I was prepared with a few questions of my own and at the appropriate time, they answered them graciously.

Before I knew it, the interview had ended. I thanked the two women for accommodating me and reinforced my deep interest in the position. We cordially said our good-byes and soon I was on my way home and feeling rather optimistic. The experi-

ence enveloped me so much that I didn't even recall
walking back through the narrow hallway. The trip
home seemed longer as I reflected on the interview
and the people I had seen and met. My interviewers
had seemed pleased, but did they like my responses?
Did I impress them? Would they hire me? For the
next two weeks, I waited. I became anxious each
time the phone rang, wanting to learn the answers
to those questions.

I had interviewed with two other companies
before this all happened and was also waiting for
a response. My wish however, was for the senior
center to call with a job offer. When the call finally
came, I immediately recognized the voice on the
other end of the line as one of the interviewers from
the senior center. My heart raced for a few seconds.
She asked whether I was still interested in the position and with controlled excitement, I responded in
the affirmative. With that said, she offered me the
position. I quickly composed myself and, ever so
calmly, accepted the offer. It was a happy moment
for me and I thought again of the people in the
large, airy room. I felt such relief, notwithstanding
some apprehension, as I thought of re-entering the
workforce. The feeling did not last very long.

By this time, it was almost a year since my family and I had moved to South Florida from the
Northeast. I took advantage of the opportunity
to care for my young daughter at home and had

thoroughly enjoyed our time together cuddling and bonding. During this time, I also learned my way around my new community. While I considered all of this a blessing, I did not want to lose connection with the world of work and its inevitable changes. With the prospect of a new job, my daily routine was about to change. I was ready for it. I was glad that this job offer came along at the time that it did and I felt comfortable about making the transition.

I quickly acclimated to my new workplace, supervisors, co-workers, and responsibilities. I must admit that this job was very different from the last job I had. At the senior center, the atmosphere was relaxed. The clients treated the employees as if we were their sons and daughters. They were never short on terms of endearment and they always had a personal story to share. I had access to a large pool of "workers" that was ready and willing to serve without compensation. The seniors insisted on staying busy and I had to be creative in matching their skills and abilities with suitable assignments, and keeping them safe and productive. Volunteer service had opened a new window of opportunity for these older adults and it was refreshing to observe how they took ownership of their responsibilities whether they worked independently or in teams.

For an entire year I stayed busy recruiting as many older adults as I could find. It was a fulfilling task. I provided training for them for various tasks, and assigned them to different organizations throughout the community. They served in various capacities and accumulated hundreds and hundreds of volunteer service hours. As the months rolled by, the number of volunteers kept increasing. I was pleasantly surprised at how many of them were willing and anxious to give back to their community. Chapter 5 of this book provides a detailed account of older adults serving as volunteers.

"One way to get the most out of life is to look upon it as an adventure."
— William Feather

A New Challenge

My role as a volunteer coordinator was fulfilling, yet I was ready for a new challenge. I contemplated other opportunities, which would still allow me to serve seniors. During this time, I was also preparing to give birth to my second child. Following much deliberation, I decided to take a six-month leave of absence, which would allow me to spend more time with my new baby and plan my next career move. Whatever I did, I realized I had very little time to decide. The pressure was on.

Looking back, I can only describe what came next as divine intervention. As I began to design my career plan, the senior center posted a job advertisement for a full-time transportation administrator. I knew right away that I could meet the job expectations and so I did not waste any time in submitting an application. Better yet, the effective start date for the job was a few months later. This could be my big break after all. Before I knew it, I was again preparing for an interview. Reflections of my first interview danced in my head, only this time I knew the territory. Remember that quaint office with the large windows at the end of the hallway? You guessed it—that's where I found myself again. I felt as if I was in a dream. Once again, the interview went well and I left with a happy and hopeful spirit.

This time, I did not have to wait very long before good news came. In fact, two pieces of good news: a job offer and a healthy baby boy! I felt that I had received a double portion of blessing in a short period of time. I made the most of the time I had caring for my two precious children, as I prepared to serve the elderly.

The morning finally came when I returned to the senior center to begin my new job. My responsibility was to provide safe and efficient transportation service to seniors who did not have access to transportation. This was a very different role, but I was ready for the challenge.

The seniors were happy to see me again and I spent time answering several questions about my newborn son. Some wanted to know when I planned on bringing him for a visit. It did not occur to me at the time how much this would mean to some of them. It was a lesson worth learning when I finally took my son to the center weeks later.

I settled into an old, but fairly comfortable chair in a shared office space with four other staff members. The office was situated in close proximity to the main entrance of the facility and had a large window. My workstation was next to the window. The advantage this piece of real estate offered was the ability to observe clients and everyone else that entered and exited the facility. It was around this time that I began to pay very close attention particularly to the seniors, observing their behaviors and habits. It was a fascinating world.

I saw them extending a helping hand to a friend or someone else they had just met. They gave each other a smile or a hug. I saw them dance and sing, and enjoy themselves. I also saw boredom and loneliness on some of their faces. Others were expressionless. At times, the seniors even fussed at each other and sometimes became belligerent. It made me wonder about them, their experiences, and just how they spent their time when they are away from the senior center, and what went through their minds as they watched and interacted with the world around them. I was in for an experience of a lifetime.

Besides the few clients who were trying to find their place in the crowd, most appeared very content to be at the senior center. For whatever reasons they visited the center, most seemed as if they were happy to be there. After all, they had paid their dues to society and it was their time to kick back, reminisce, and enjoy each other's company and friendship as they grew older.

I noticed that the seniors seemed willing to try new things, which is not always the case with older adults. I soon realized that the senior center and what it represented had provided them an opportunity to express themselves in ways they might not have, under different circumstances. It created a new life, a new world for most, if not all of them. They knew how to laugh at themselves and not really be concerned about the opinions of others. More and more I felt myself being drawn into their world.

This journey, this experience, has provided new perspectives, new expectations, and yes, new appreciation for older people. I have chosen to stay on this journey for there is much to learn as I think of older relatives and friends, and myself at that stage of life.

Less than two years into the job, it was evident that the clientele at the center was steadily increasing. So was the need for more services, more equipment, a bigger staff, and of course, a larger facility. We were bursting at the seams and a move was imminent. Even the clients had noticed the change and I heard them discussing the issue from time to time. The community was responding to the availability of essential services at little or no cost to them. There was every reason for residents and visitors to take advantage of these services.

The City was already preparing to respond to the need and construction of a new senior center was soon in progress. It was amazing how well the staff and clients coped with the limited space. About a year later, the new facility was completed. It was an imposing structure, which almost quadrupled the old facility. In fact, there was no comparison. It could not have come at a better time as plans for expanded services were already in full swing.

The entire senior center community was excited about the "big move." A change was coming. It was much like preparing to move into a new home and a new community. I believe the seniors were more excited than anybody else, as they knew the transition would enhance their experience. It took several days to move and set up equipment, furnishings, and other items in the new facility. Both clients and staff were ecstatic about occupying the new space, but I was especially proud of the joy this would bring to many who understood the significance of this change.

> "Follow your bliss and doors will open for you that you never knew existed. Follow your bliss and the universe will open doors for you where there were only walls."
> – Joseph Campbell

The Principals

Through the thin, green slots of the blinds that hugged my new office window, I saw them carefully disembarking the city vehicles used to transport them.

Picture this: one by one men and women exit the vehicles. Their driver gives them a helping hand to safely get from the steps of the vehicle to solid ground. Some smile at the driver. Others talk to their friends, while some seem preoccupied. The driver takes their bags or purses to make their exit easier and safer. They purposefully make their way toward the main entrance of the center. A few seniors in wheelchairs get special assistance in disembarking the vehicle. The driver lowers the lift carrying the client, then with care and precision she rolls the chair toward the entrance of the building. This process continues until every vehicle safely delivers its passengers. The process reverses itself in the afternoon when the seniors head back home.

As the seniors headed toward the building, I noticed that some walked slowly, clutching their personal effects—a pocket book, a bag, or even a small suitcase. I often wondered what was inside those suitcases, but never had the courage to ask. Some even "carried" their walking canes that are supposed to help support their bodies. This practice was puzzling at first. Shouldn't they be using the canes for support? I still wonder about that. Some seniors moved briskly as if they were late for an appointment. I noticed that some of them chatted happily with each other as they walked along and their gestures often made me smile. Others gingerly made their way toward the entrance of the facility with the help of a friend. After all, what's the hurry? They had all day.

As I scoured their faces, I detected a smile on some, a stern disposition on others, and some sported a grimace as they made their way inside the building. Occasionally, one or two seniors would stop and sit on a bench to rest a while and catch their breath. The caring spirit of some of the seniors was evident as they stopped and waited for the ones sitting on the benches. One by one they made their way into the warm and cozy environment of the senior center.

A few seniors were fortunate to have the means to transport themselves to the center. Others had friends or relatives who transported them. By whatever means they came to the center and despite the countless visits they made, their attitude seemed to suggest they were visiting for the first time. The facial expressions of most of the clients confirmed their enthusiasm about attending the center, and I soon realized that many considered the center a home away from home; a sanctuary. Some seniors attended the center once or twice per week, others attended multiple days per week. I am convinced that if some of them had the opportunity, they would attend more often.

The well-appointed lobby of the senior center was an expansive area. It was often bathed in the warm Florida sunshine courtesy of the impressive skylights in the cathedral ceiling. A friendly receptionist managed the attractive and ample reception desk. She had a warm personality and made an effort to greet everyone who passed by the desk. The space was beautifully decorated with plush furnishings and tasteful wall hangings, which the seniors enjoyed. A few older adults would pause at the desk en route to the main hall. They would attempt to converse with the receptionist even when it was evident that she was busy attending to visitors or taking and transferring phone messages. Eventually, they would make their way toward their usual and customary spot. Every senior had their usual and customary space; like many of us, they are creatures of habit.

On their first visit to the new center, the seniors seemed overwhelmed by the sheer size of the facility. It truly was enormous–they almost needed a map to navigate the multiple rooms. This place was much different from the old place. No longer were the rooms a few steps away. They had no choice but to walk a little farther to get from one area to the next. For those who used an electric scooter, it was an adventure. The senior center staff and some caring volunteers who had already familiarized themselves with the layout of the facility were on hand to assist and direct the seniors. It was necessary.

It is true that older adults do not acclimate quickly to most life changes. This was one of them. One could see the reluctance on some of their faces as they slowly ambulated. They did not want to be bothered. I suppose, however, that this group of seniors eventually concluded that the benefits far outweighed the extra effort they had to make to get around. It took them a while, but day-by-day they made progress in navigating the center.

With the exception of the new clients, one could easily see that the seniors had established a daily routine upon arrival at the center. Most clients immediately secured their meal ticket for the day's sumptuous fare that was delivered each day by a catering firm. They were responsible for ordering their meals by the deadline and while there was not a charge for the meals, the clients were expected to make a donation. Each client had to inform the on-site nutritionist of their desire to have lunch on the days that they planned on visiting the center.

Typically, the number of lunches delivered on any given day was the number of lunches that seniors had ordered. Subsequently, any client who failed to order a lunch ran the risk of not getting lunch through the program. This did not mean that clients would not eat if they neglected to order their lunch. There were other places in the center that served food, but it came at a cost. Thankfully, daily cancellations of client trips to the center meant there were always lunches available. Additionally, clients had the option of purchasing a hot or cold snack from the center's gift shop, which stocked plenty of goodies. If a client could not afford to purchase their own food, staff would intervene and assist. Absolutely no senior went unfed at the senior center.

Once the seniors secured their meal tickets, the next stop for most of them was the coffee stand to get a hot beverage. This was an event. There they had a chance to purchase a freshly brewed cup of coffee or tea for only a quarter—a quarter! It gets even better. Coffee was served free to everyone whenever a senior celebrated his or her birthday. As you can well imagine, as many seniors who regularly attended the center, there was a birthday celebration every day—or so it seemed. What a treat!

They would congregate at coffee tables in a section of the main hall sipping the hot drink as they chatted with each other. Occasionally an unstable hand would cause the hot beverage to spill on their clothing. No one was ever in danger from such an incident; they just had to live with coffee stains on their clothes for the remainder of the day. The seniors who were not having coffee or tea would head toward the main hall to get comfortable at their favorite table. This seemed like a ritual. Older adults tend to be territorial and some are sometimes possessive. They were neither hesitant nor bashful about expressing their feelings either. Once they had established their favorite spot at one of the large round tables, they would take ownership of that space and expect it to be available to them each time.

Some seniors took it a step further—they marked their chair with a place card, a bag, or any personal item, which was best left untouched. Seniors who were less concerned about where they sat, or who were unaware of the practice, ran the risk of learning a lesson the hard way. I stood perplexed for a few moments the first time I witnessed a nasty argument when one senior unwittingly took another's chair and then decided to stay put. I just did not expect this kind of behavior from adults, and older adults to boot. Shouldn't they know better? Senior center counselors and social workers would have to intervene in order to restore calm and order during such events. Thankfully, they came infrequently.

Little by little, as the morning wore on, the large, empty, round tables seemed to disappear with the arrival of the seniors. Generally the first few minutes were spent in friendly and exciting chatter; or for some, a quiet moment as each person prepared for the day's activities.

Each day, the seniors arrived dressed in an array of styles. Some wore bright colored clothing. Some wore pretty pastels, while others wore basic black or white. Not to be left out were the ones who, for whatever reason, wore a combination of plaid and striped clothing. Admittedly, some of the styles were outdated. Some of the women seemed trapped in one time period. They seemed to forget that while fashion and style repeat themselves, they often get made over with different fabrics and cuts.

It was no surprise, however, that a large percentage of seniors adorned themselves in more trendy styles. Their clothing ranged from crisp, tailor-made outfits and tastefully coordinated pieces, to sporty and simple styles. Their wardrobe included ruffles, lace detailing, jeans with the trouser cut, and other fashion trends. The look was complete with accessories: big, chunky jewelry and fashionable handbags. A handful of women who seemed to want to maintain what's left of their youthful appearance, regularly wore above-the-knee length skirts and dresses. This choice in fashion drew the attention of many, especially members of the opposite sex, and often became a topic of discussion.

At this senior center, participants were required to be sixty years or older to be eligible for services. This requirement was later changed to fifty-five years or older. If a spouse was just approaching the age requirement, he or she would be allowed to register. In other words, they would be grandfathered in. The average age of the client population was around seventy and there were more women than men. The diverse client population comprised Blacks, Caucasians, Hispanics, Asians, Indians, and other groups.

There were many nationalities represented as well. A few minutes spent listening to these individuals revealed the many different languages they spoke: English, Spanish, French, Creole, Italian, Hebrew, German, Portuguese, Mandarin Chinese, and one or two other languages that I might not have recognized. This blending of cultures—language, thoughts, communication styles, customs, beliefs, attitudes, and values—made for a rich experience for just about everyone. What a great opportunity it was to interact with these older adults and to get a glimpse into their backgrounds.

What's In a Senior Center?

Senior centers are important community-based gathering places that provide a warm, safe, and friendly atmosphere for everyone who enters through their doors. Senior centers come in all shapes and sizes. They provide many free programs and services, which allow social contact and community for individuals who might otherwise feel isolated. Each new day allows an opportunity for many seniors to visit the senior center. Hundreds visit daily, immersing themselves in the many different activities offered, or just finding a comfortable spot and watching the day go by. This senior center that I described offered its participants an array of services and activities that captivated their interests and kept them thoroughly engaged. It remains an enviable program.

Senior Centers

The senior center concept was first introduced in New York City in 1943 to provide social activities, nutritious meals, and case management to older adults age sixty and older, especially individuals with low incomes. Since that time, senior centers have become important focal points in their communities.

According to the National Institute of Senior Centers (NISC), there are approximately 11,000 senior centers around the country serving almost 1 million older adults daily from all walks of life. While there are varying types of senior centers, they all function to enhance the lives of older adults physically, intellectually, spiritually, and socially. They provide a means for mature adults to age with dignity, security, and purpose within their communities.

Over the years, senior centers have expanded and redefined their role in society. They provide volunteer opportunities, meaningful work, transportation services, and access to valuable benefits and resources. Another important milestone for senior centers is receiving national accreditation status. To be awarded this prestigious status, senior centers must meet nine standards of excellence as established by the National Institute of Senior Centers. The standards include purpose, community, governance, administration and human resources, program planning, evaluation, fiscal management, record and reports, and facility management.

All efforts toward accreditation are driven by hard work and commitment and ensure that senior centers provide the highest level of service and care for the elderly in our community.

The older adults who attended the senior center described in this book did so for various reasons. Most were seeking an opportunity to socialize. They refused to stay home alone. At the center, they found countless opportunities to meet and greet different people while enhancing their quality of life.

The center was the place for the elderly to connect and they did just that. This is where they forged lasting relationships—relationships that have added years to the lives of some. Seniors befriended each other and many looked out for each other, whether it was on the bus, at lunch, in a classroom, or elsewhere, it was evident that they shared a lot.

Very often I would hear comments such as, "I get so bored being at home by myself; I have to get out."

"I can only watch so much television or take so many naps; I'd rather be here."

"Why should I stay home and look at the four walls?"

"This place has saved my life!"

"What, are you kidding me? I wish I could come to this place every single day!"

Like any other social group, the seniors quickly formed small friendship groups or they moved about in pairs. There were a few loners. Some seniors developed long-term relationships while visiting the center. In fact, some very intimate relationships came about as a result of the camaraderie that developed. You can bet that any such happenings became the top-of-the-hour news instantly.

Other seniors enjoyed the myriad of activities that were offered, such as arts and crafts, ceramics, computers, sewing, bingo, current events, lectures and much, much more. They participated in one or more activities, which filled their day and engaged their minds.

Some clients simply wanted to enjoy the warm, open atmosphere at the center as they could relax comfortably in the large, plush couches and chairs that furnished the building. From their comfortable posts they absorbed themselves in the activities around them.

I noticed that whenever a staff member walked by, some of the seniors would look up—their eager faces suggesting that they expected a friendly greeting, or even a smile. I made an effort to greet them whenever I passed by, and oftentimes it would be the same individual several times throughout the day. At first thought, this appeared to be a simple gesture, but I soon realized it was a gesture that the seniors appreciated and that meant a lot to them. For an older person, especially one who is new to the senior center life, it made a world of difference.

Sometimes the friendly greeting appeared to help them muster up the courage to start a conversation. To have someone show interest in them was a delight. They enjoyed talking and if I allowed them, some would talk for hours on end. I was trapped in conversation on many occasions and I recall having to politely excuse myself. I regretted having to end some of the conversations, especially when they were gushing over their children or grandchildren or what they did when they were young professionals. It is not because I did not care about what the seniors had to say; I really wanted to be gracious and share in their joy, and I did that most of the times. I felt satisfied that I was able to balance my obligations at work with accommodating them when I could.

A handful of seniors took advantage of the cozy library decorated just for them. Its dark cherry wood furnishings gave the spacious room a warm and soothing feel. The floor-to-ceiling bookshelves were impressive and filled with magazines, novels, how-to booklets, encyclopedias, and the daily newspapers. The couches and chairs looked inviting. The library patrons seemed not to be in any hurry as they moved almost methodically from one shelf to the next trying to settle on something of interest. A few seniors sat comfortably reading a book or newspaper or thumbing through the pages of a magazine. Others seemed to have gotten so comfortable, they fell asleep or maybe they were meditating; I never stopped to check.

The scene always brought a smile to my face and then at times I envied them, especially when I considered my busy schedule, my workload and how much juggling I had to do in order to meet personal and work obligations. I, too, wished that I could join them and enjoy a moment of peace and harmony. What was I thinking? I had to remind myself that these individuals had earned the right to take life easy. They share common experiences and have now reached the stage in their lives where they can slow down and not take life too seriously. I am yet to get to that stage.

Nonetheless, it was surprising to see how many of them were eager to assist with various activities at the center. They wanted to participate in activities that would engage their hands and intellect. They were in the right place and exposed to a multitude of volunteer opportunities.

Regardless of their reasons for attending the senior center, one thing was clear: this choice added purpose and meaning to their lives.

Older Adults as Volunteers

Volunteering is a treasured resource! Volunteers were the backbone of the senior center during the time I worked there. There were over 300 senior volunteers assisting in many different roles. They were so dedicated and enthusiastic about their responsibilities that they showed up everyday as if they were working for a salary. For these individuals, however, it was a much larger mission.

In addition to giving back to their community, volunteering empowers older adults and provides a wholesome sense of satisfaction and confidence. State and local networks of organizations and leaders have relied on the support of volunteers. Volunteers have been significant contributors to aging services networks, serving at every level and in the delivery of all types of services. When volunteers serve, their efforts significantly benefit the community, the organization, and the volunteer. When they give their time, talent, wisdom, and experience, they are largely giving back to their community. They are making a difference by being part of a national movement to transform America through the involvement of its citizens.

By donating their time and skills, older adults are saving money for the organizations they serve, and helping to make funds go further. Through service, they are also adding to the quality and health of their lives. Research shows that when seniors volunteer, they keep their minds and body active, and help improve their cognitive abilities.

At the senior center, there was no doubt about whether the volunteers developed new friendships, stayed active, learned new skills, and kept better health. Whatever their experience and abilities were, there was a senior volunteer position for every interested person. From tour guides to servers, office helpers to music makers, they made their presence felt.

GREETERS

At the senior center, there was a group of older adults who were always poised and ready to welcome new members. They took pride in carrying out this critical function of the initiation process of all seniors. Their warm smiles and kind greetings were enough to put a nervous soul at ease. They introduced new members to staff and other clients. They gave personal tours of the facility, pointing out all the important and essential amenities and services that were available. This gesture helped seniors acclimate quickly to their new surroundings and proved to be an excellent opportunity for them to start building new friendships.

Gift Shop Associates

Another group of seniors managed the beautifully decorated gift shop at the center. They worked in shifts and executed their duties as if they were partners operating their own private business. The space was well lit, the shelves neatly and abundantly stocked. There were baskets of fruits and healthy treats next to packets of candy and energy bars. A variety of juices and sodas filled the large drink refrigerator. There was something for everyone.

There was also enough room inside the gift shop for a few small tables and chairs where patrons dined. This arrangement added to the ambience. In fact, as the months went by, staff set up tables and chairs just outside the gift shop, giving patrons the feeling of dining "al fresco." It seemed to me the patrons were doing more talking and little dining, but it didn't matter; it brought them together and gave them a chance to interact in a pleasant and casual atmosphere.

Back inside the gift shop, there was a greeting for everyone who entered. Senior volunteers assisted shoppers with their selections, and were prompt to assist with simple food preparation, such as microwaving a beef patty or a cup of soup. In this gift shop, there were no cash registers. Instead, the workers armed themselves with note pads on which they did calculations when necessary and recorded transactions throughout the day. The process was slow sometimes, but no one seemed to mind. It was all part of the experience. Occasionally, one of the workers would pull out a calculator to help speed up the process.

COFFEE STATION ATTENDANTS

The coffee station was a separate operation and also a busy corner especially during the mornings. Seniors loved volunteering in this area. Every morning, they set up a huge coffee maker and a tea maker for the tea lovers. Like players on a football team each senior had a specific task. Each morning, the volunteers took up their positions and put a smile on their face; ready to serve their peers. They neatly displayed the small packets of tea, sugar, creamers, stirrers, napkins, and Styrofoam cups, which they replenished throughout the morning.

As the seniors interacted with one another at the coffee station, they positioned themselves yet again for an opportunity to develop new friendships. The volunteers greeted everyone with, "Good morning, what would you like–coffee or tea?"

The response would be followed by, "Do you have it black or would you like cream and sugar?"

In seconds the hot beverage of choice was served and a quarter later, everyone was enjoying coffee or tea. Before they cleaned up the coffee station and set the stage for the next day, the volunteers consulted with the transportation staff to verify that all the buses had dropped off the seniors for that day.

Lunch Bunch

Senior volunteers also assisted with preparations for the daily lunches. Like clockwork, every morning they set up a production line. It was fascinating to watch! A small group of seniors neatly arranged brightly colored serving trays in one area of the main hall which doubled as a dining room. Another group wrapped the plastic silverware in napkins, while another group placed the wrapped silverware on the trays. As soon as the daily lunch packets were delivered, the volunteers worked feverishly to place them on the trays, just in time for lunch. Once everyone was served, all the seniors who had ordered lunch readied themselves to eat, but not before singing the national anthem: "God Bless America."

Every day as I sat in my office I could hear the group belting out the song with pride. I must admit that sometimes the rendition was so dissonant it hurt the ears. Nonetheless, they sang from their hearts and they knew every word of that song. Their renditions were no worse than those of a few of today's pop artists who do an injustice to the song in front of millions. I cringe each time the news media remind us of such performance blunders. The singing of "God Bless America" was followed by a short prayer led by one of the seniors.

Finally, it was time to eat and the seniors who had brought their own lunches joined in. While lunch was not haute cuisine, the food was fresh, healthy, and nutritious. Seniors enjoyed vegetarian entrees, beef, poultry, fish, and pasta entrees. They also enjoyed a variety of soups, breads and dessert items. For some seniors, this lunch was the most substantial meal of the day. This might be their sole reason for visiting the senior center. While some seniors finished all of their meal, others did not. In some instances, I believe this was due to the selection for the day that just did not appeal to some seniors.

In any case, before everyone was finished with their meal, there was another group of volunteers who were poised to move in and help clean up after the lunch crowd. They took their responsibilities seriously, going from table to table gathering plates, leftover foods, utensils, and Styrofoam cups, which they tossed into large garbage bags. They kept this up until all the tables were clean and the huge space was back to functioning as the main hall.

ACTIVITY DESK HELPERS

The activity desk was often abuzz with seniors ready for the next adventure. This was the station where they registered for various activities hosted by the center, including trips, special functions, parties, and other events. At the activity desk, one could find the latest copy of the center's monthly calendar with a listing of ongoing and upcoming events as well as useful phone numbers and other resources. Here, volunteers and staff assistants verified memberships, documented names, collected cash for events that required a fee, distributed receipts, and provided additional information.

Some events were sold out almost immediately and often required staff to place seniors on a wait list. Oh, that dreaded wait list! This was never a fun time; not for seniors, nor volunteers, nor staff members. No one wanted to be placed on any wait list. It made them feel left out or being denied an opportunity. This alternative made for some anxious moments for many seniors and some who did not always respond kindly. This is the time some of them displayed their ugly side. I have seen tempers flare like a blazing fire, leaving volunteers and staff to exercise patience and diplomacy while attempting to calm emotions and offering explanations and assuring words to dissatisfied clients. Staff always found a way to resolve the issues as they presented themselves.

SONGBIRDS

The Songbirds, as they were called, always had music on their mind and a song in their heart. They were a diverse group of volunteers who enjoyed singing and performing in front of a crowd. They were compassionate artists who donated their time and talent for a good cause. They rehearsed every week and regularly showcased their talents at local nursing homes, assisted living facilities, and special events in the community. Their performances and positive outlook helped to improve their quality of life as well as the quality of life for many others, especially persons with Alzheimer's disease.

Whenever the songbirds performed for their peers, the response always warmed my heart. On many occasions the clients who attended the Alzheimer's program at the center joined the general population to enjoy the festivities. Most of them sported an expectant look and even those who seemed disinterested at first responded to the sound of the music. Their eager and smiling faces told the story. As the performers harmonized, one could not help but think that it provided an escape from the sadness or worry that some of their peers felt. It reduced their stress and anxiety even for a while. I smiled as I watched some of these individuals, including seniors in their wheelchairs, clapping out of rhythm or trying to sing along. Looking at these individuals and the timeless expressions on their faces, reminded me every time that I should offer up more praise and less complaints.

All throughout the year, the songbirds shared their passion. They had a special program for each season. However, I believe they had more fun during the Christmas season. They found pleasure in going from office to office singing Christmas carols and holiday jingles. They harmonized well and no one could contain their enthusiasm. These older adults were doing something that they enjoyed and best of all they were enriching the lives of other people.

TEACHERS AND ARTISTS

There were other seniors who took great pride in sharing their professional and vocational accomplishments. They readily shared the skills they had acquired over the years and offered advice to anyone who was interested. They did so through participation in various activities such as support groups and hands-on activities including sewing, arts and crafts, ceramics, cooking and dancing, and more.

The support groups provided a safe and comfortable setting in which older adults could interact. With a member of staff facilitating the activity, each person was given a chance to participate in the discussions. The seniors were eager and completely uninhibited in sharing their experiences— good and bad. It was an exercise that gave many of them a chance to revisit their past and its many memories. In many ways, they realized how much they had in common.

The artistic abilities of some of these seniors shone in the artwork they produced. From beautifully decorated pillows and colorful afghans to exquisite ceramic pieces, they showcased their talents and held nothing back. They frequently met in small groups and with all the tools of the trade, cut, assembled, stitched together, and embellished the pieces that later resulted in items that were ready for any showroom.

Whenever I had a chance to observe these individuals, they just seemed to get lost in the tasks at hand. It was fun for most, therapy for others and a wonderful way to build confidence and good relations. Besides gushing over what brought them joy, it was a chance for them to demonstrate their philanthropic spirit by donating some of their works of art. Not only were they helping themselves, the fruits of their labor were benefiting others.

It was at the senior center that I got a lesson in the art of ceramics. I had always seen the end product, but never knew all the intricacies involved in producing the beautiful ceramic pieces. The first time I surveyed the workshop, I was immediately drawn in. It was furnished with all the equipment needed to create the pieces. There were drying racks that housed several pottery pieces waiting for the next stage. Next to the racks was what looked like a kiln. I would later learn the purpose of such equipment. On a table in the corner were mounds of clay body.

The seniors used the clay body to form objects of different shapes. First, they had to knead the clay body in order to evenly distribute the moisture content. Who knew? It seemed like a tedious task, but they made it look simple. At this stage, these objects, or greenware as they are called, had to go through a firing process to remove moisture and set the shape of the object. The firing was done in the kiln! The seniors decorated the ware in beautiful and distinctive motifs. From vases to cups and bowls, they proudly showcased their artwork.

The participation of these older adults in the various activities confirms the value of their accomplishments and contributions to society. For them, the benefits were twofold: they felt pride in sharing their time and talents with others and they had fun along the way. This demonstration of service to others could be a great lesson, particularly for today's youth.

Older Workers in the Labor Force

While many older adults volunteer in and around their community, the reality is that today, they are increasingly retiring later in life or rejoining the workforce. The U.S. Bureau of Labor Statistics reports that the number of workers between the ages of 65 and 74 and those aged 75 and older are expected to increase more than 80 percent. It is also expected that workers age 65 and up will account for 6.1 percent of the total labor force; a sharp increase from 3.6 percent in 2006.

These statistics are staggering! Just look around you and you will find older workers in the fields of education, transportation, trade, utilities, health services, as well as business and professional services. They tend to be more task-oriented and they are more disciplined in their conduct on the job. No wonder many employers are embracing this group. It is easy to determine whether a business is more accepting of older workers; look for these clues:

- They offer on-the-job training
- They hire for temporary work assignments
- They offer flexible work schedules, including opportunities to work from

If you are an elderly worker, sharpen your skills and empower yourself by staying informed about workplace changes and development. Ask family members, friends, and colleagues about training opportunities in your community. Visit your local One-Stop Career Centers or check out the resources available to seniors on the Senior Community Service Employment Program (SCSEP) website at www.doleta.gov/seniors/.

Source: U.S. Bureau of Labor Statistics (www.bls.com)

Seniors at Play

I think you will agree with me when I say that seniors know how to have fun. Remember, they were once kids! Yes, they never ceased to amaze me and occasionally, I would find myself identifying a few individuals whom I thought I would want to emulate. My observation of older adults, to some degree, gives me a peek into how I might behave in later years. Allow me to take you on a journey of seniors at play at the senior center.

During my time there, I noticed that whenever there was a celebration of any kind, one could expect to see a large representation of seniors. They all showed up for varying reasons: they wanted to participate in the fun, they did not want to be excluded, or they had nothing else to do. In most cases, they just wanted to share in the fun. One event that simply fascinated me, and the seniors as well, was International Day. The International Day celebration was truly a time to recognize the diversity of the elderly population and observe how their cultural differences enriched their lives.

INTERNATIONAL DAY

One could tell right away that it was International Day once the seniors got off the buses that transported them. They looked even more colorful than any other day of the week dressed in their national threads of varied designs, textures, colors, and layers. Attendance on this day was generally higher, too. The smiles on the faces of both men and women reflected their pride, enthusiasm and patriotism. They were proud to represent their respective countries and it showed as they made their way into the facility.

Staff dedicated several months to planning and coordinating this special day. It was a center-wide event. The result was an entire day filled with music, dancing, a fashion show, and of course, a sampling of foods from the different cultures. It truly was exciting to observe. The wide stage in the main hall was tastefully decorated in preparation for a fashion show that was always a big attraction. Ethnic music filled the air and excitement among the group began to build as the seniors got dressed for the fashion show. Some employees and other onlookers stopped to take it all in. The judges positioned themselves at a nearby table and the photographers readied their cameras as the audience eagerly awaited.

Almost as soon as a staff member had given the welcome and special announcements, the participating seniors started forming a line to go on stage. They stood in order of the individual countries they each represented. Most could not keep still as they waited. They made last minute checks of their hair and clothing while chatting and smiling nervously with their peers.

The change in the tempo of the music signaled the start of the event. The announcer, microphone in hand, belted out the name of the first contestant along with a brief description and the contestant proudly made her way on to the stage. The audience roared! For about an hour or so, country by country and with accompanying music that represented each country, the seniors carefully mounted the steps that took them on to the beautifully decorated and well-lit stage. I was pleasantly surprised to see that they were not bashful in displaying their talents, and some were very talented.

As they danced to the beat of the music some moved deliberately and passionately across the stage showing off their costumes and dance moves. Others danced their way across the stage swinging their hips from side to side and sometimes stopping to bow or curtsy. An occasional laughter from the audience punctuated the air. They cheered and encouraged the contestants along. Their energy level was really high on this day.

It did not matter that a handful of seniors seemed rhythmically challenged as they took the spotlight.

They were not deterred at all. Some seniors were so caught up in their performance that they seemed to forget they were only allowed a brief time on stage and so they lingered as if savoring the moment. A few of them seemed to shuffle across the stage, while others seemed a bit out of breath. Nonetheless, they were enjoying themselves and even for that brief moment, performing in front of their peers invigorated them—at least, so it seemed.

Just like their grand entrance on to the stage, they each made a less than subtle exit, pausing only to be photographed. They gave big wide smiles. It was a "Hollywood moment" for them. The show continued until every senior had a chance to participate. It was a beautiful scene to watch.

Like celebrities, once they got back into the general population, they approached and greeted their friends and family members who had attended the event. Small groups dotted the main hall. The seniors took even more photographs. Their poses were hilarious as some seniors tried to outdo the others. Some allowed a close up shot of their outfits taking every opportunity to explain its significance. The fun did not end there as the seniors continued the celebration with food and drinks. There was a wide display of ethnic foods for the seniors to enjoy. The best part was that it was free! They ate, chatted, and laughed among themselves. What a proud and happy people they were!

Independence Day

Independence Day celebration was yet another opportunity to watch seniors at play. In a spirit of patriotism, they came to the center donned in their red, white and blue outfits. Some brought along miniature flags, which they waved periodically, while others wore flag lapel pins on their clothing. Not to be outdone were several members of staff who also dressed for the occasion. Even the towering columns that stood in the lobby were decorated with red, white and blue ribbons. The veterans among the senior population were especially proud and seemed to have a little pep in their steps on that day.

No July Fourth holiday would be complete without a barbeque at the center. Senior volunteers and staff took to the covered back patio in the Florida summer heat, hovering over big grills filled with hotdogs and burgers. Many flips, and a few flops later, everyone was getting their hands and fingers dirty enjoying a delicious hotdog or burger served with chips, baked beans, a slice of cake or brownie on the side, and a beverage. Delicious! It was definitely not the time to count calories. The seniors were also entertained with music and dancing as they enjoyed their lunch. Together, employees and clients immersed themselves in the day's festivities.

INDOOR HORSE RACING

Each year, one of the most watched and most exciting events at the center was indoor horse racing. The race that you are about to "see" was dubbed the "Geritol Downs." The race really got my attention the first time I saw it. I will set the stage for readers who are not familiar with indoor horse racing. Imagine this! Staff and senior volunteers arranged colorful, wooden horses that stood almost three feet high on a long and ample sheet of thick paper. There were multiple lanes clearly and neatly marked on the paper. The lanes were numbered and so were the wooden horses. Bold lines outlining boxes in each lane created a holding place for the horses and allowed the jockeys, played by seniors and employees, to physically advance and position their horses as their numbers were called. The horses had names such as "Johnny Be Good," "My 401K Plan," "My Bread and Butter," and "Shalimar."

Before the race began, seniors who wanted to bet on the horses got in line at the ticket booth to secure their tickets. The cost was a whopping twenty-five cents per horse. Tickets in hand, the seniors who were betting on the horses and other eager spectators "filled the stands" and lined both sides of the staging area, sitting comfortably and waiting anxiously for the race to begin. The jockeys positioned themselves to "ride" their horses. The jockeys would advance their horses when their number was called.

The announcer for the races got in place, along with an assistant. The race was set to begin, but as the announcer was about to call the first race, a few late comers yelled for him to wait while they got their tickets. Reluctantly, the announcer waited. As the late comers seated themselves, they were greeted with a few mean stares from impatient spectators. The announcer resumed his duty.

At the starting bell, the announcer screamed, "They're off!" The jockeys gently prodded their horses. The announcer started pulling numbers at random.

"And it's My Bread and Butter moving up!" "Eleven, here comes number eleven, and on its heels is number four, number four!" The onlookers cheered and laughed.

"Watch out, number six, here comes Johnny Be Good!" yelled the announcer.

"And number eight is about to take the lead!"

"C'mon, c'mon!" one jockey yelled.

"Look out for number six!" the announcer screamed again. As he screamed the numbers, the jockeys who had still not left the starting gate, waited impatiently to hear their number called so they could advance. Soon all the horses had taken to the track and were headed for the finish line.

Meanwhile the crowd roared as the horses "galloped" from across the hall.

"My horse is gonna win, man!" one man shouted to his neighbor.

"Quiet, you!" his opponent yelled back.

Just then the announcer shouted and beckoned to number nine who at that moment was running neck and neck with number eight. By this time several seniors had gotten out of their seats and were yelling the names of their prized horses.

"My Bread and Butter, c'mon, baby!" another jockey urged.

"My 401K Plan, I'm counting on you!" yelled another.

"Don't let me down, Shalimar!" a female jockey shrieked.

A couple of the jockeys did not show much emotion; they seemed to be willing their horses along as they looked around nervously. It was easy to spot the pros among the contestants. The yelling, screaming, cheering, and laughing continued throughout the entire race. By then there were a couple horses that were only yards away from the finish line. Finally the announcer screamed for the winner, "It's number nine; number nine, ride on down!"

The jockey riding My Bread and Butter proudly made his way across the finish line to the roar of the spectators. Those who had betted on the horse screamed the loudest. They jumped to their feet, if they were not standing by then, cheering loudly and giving each other high fives. The jockey beamed and gently patted his horse while trying to do a victory lap.

Meanwhile, the losers griped, but remained in good spirit as they prepared for the next race. Soon the winners began to form a line to collect their winnings—grinning all the way. They purchased more tickets. Several seniors decided to stay with the same horses for good luck. Several exciting races later, the Geritol Downs had come to an end.

Seniors gathered around and chatted excitedly about the races. Some had a few quarters less; others had more. Nonetheless, it was a fun experience for everyone and for that hour or longer, it was a joy to watch these seniors at play and having fun.

ART AT WORK

The sound of children almost always got the attention of older adults at the senior center. They looked forward to every chance to engage in activities with children. From time to time, children from schools in the community toured the senior center. The seniors always seemed delighted to see them. One year, I had an opportunity to volunteer in the Kids and the Power of Work Program (KAPOW). I volunteered at a local elementary school and visited the same fifth grade class on more than one occasion. I was also their host when they came to tour the senior center.

As planned, the large group of students arrived on time at the center in a bright yellow school bus. They were smiling as they anxiously alighted from the vehicle. I went out and met their teacher and a chaperone who carefully shepherded the students off the vehicle. The students immediately formed a neat line. Before entering the building, the teacher and chaperone reminded the students to be on their best behavior. As they quietly marched into the building, they immediately became the focus of everyone's attention. Many of the seniors who were seated or walking in the lobby smiled and waved at the students. The students waved back. Some seniors uttered kind words to the children as they passed by. A few employees came out of their offices to see and greet the children. I escorted the group to a waiting area and provided them with a few preliminary instructions and gave them an idea of how they would spend their time.

I wanted to be sure the students would maximize their time during the tour, and so I sought approval in advance from the instructor of the Art class to have the young students join them for a few minutes. Following the briefing and a few questions, I ushered the students into the classroom just as the seniors—all women, were setting up their workstations. There were six seniors and the students got in small groups to watch each senior do what they enjoyed most. As they got started on their work of art, I walked from table to table observing the activity. I tried keeping the students quiet as they had started conversing with the artists.

I finally stopped a while at the workstation of a client who frequently visited the transportation office to make arrangements for her trips. I often admired her; a slender build, woman who stood at least 5' 7" tall and carried herself in a sophisticated manner. She moved with unbelievable poise and grace and no one would guess that she is ninety-something. I also often wondered what she carried in that neat, opaque satchel by her side. She never seemed to leave home without it. As I stood there watching her, it all made sense to me.

As she methodically positioned her tools, she showed us the picture that she was about to capture in her painting. She smiled warmly at the students and then without delay, she began painting. With delicate movements of her hand and fingers and meticulous strokes, she began to produce the scene on the paper.

She was completely absorbed in the task at hand as I watched in complete amazement. The students were equally impressed as they stared at the paper. As she painted, she stopped periodically to speak to them. She spoke in a deliberate yet soft and controlled tone. After a few minutes, a student asked her a question about the painting. Soon the senior was fielding questions from a number of them. She responded in an easy and simple fashion so that the students would understand.

As the minutes ticked away, a cluster of beautiful and colorful flowers began to appear beneath the paintbrush. The outline of each petal was subtle yet well defined in just the right areas. The colors were varied shades of light and dark green, yellow and orange, and seemed to leap off the surface of the paper. The students shuffled around so that they could get a good look at the painting. With a few more strokes of the paintbrush, the senior created a beautiful piece of artwork. It was a beautiful bouquet of flowers.

Upon completing the painting, she held it up high enough for everyone to see and with a look of pride and satisfaction, she showed off her handiwork to the students. It was beautiful! It truly was a learning experience and a pleasant experience for everyone as we looked on in admiration.

During that time the rest of the seniors had produced some eye-catching pieces as well. We went from table to table admiring the pieces. The seniors even allowed some of the students to get some hands-on practice. The students were eager to participate and quickly got into action. When they left, some walked away smiling with pieces of artwork that they had created. Some left with artwork that the seniors had given them. As they walked out of the room, I watched them admiring their own artwork, showing them off, or comparing them with their classmates'. What a lasting impression the experience had left on these young minds.

TECHNOLOGY AT PLAY

Seniors today are speeding along the information highway and they are embracing high-tech gadgets, such as iPads and other tablets. Look around you and you will see baby-boomers cradling cellphones, laptops, or game consoles. Technology has provided new ways for seniors to stay in touch with family and friends, regardless of location, and opens up another avenue for seniors to interact and stay current. Many are online surfing the Internet and sending and receiving emails as well as photographs of family members. They are also involved with social networking sites such as Facebook and Twitter and they are blogging and Skyping. Imagine that grandparents are now Skyping their grandchildren instead of writing and sending letters to them!

I saw several seniors enrolling in Computer classes at the senior center. Some of them had never even used a computer, let alone know what a mouse is and does in this context. For many, reading the screen or navigating did not come easily, but they were eager to learn. Not only are seniors taking advantage of the classes offered at senior centers in their communities, they are frequenting their local libraries to use the resources there.

The adoption of technology by older adults is a choice for some and a necessity for others. There are still some who refuse to embrace technology. However, with so many consumer services at their fingertips and information that affect their daily lives, more and more seniors are drawn to this new way of life. The trend is bound to increase.

INTERGENERATIONAL PROGRAM

The intergenerational program at the center brought seniors and young children together for play time and story time. Parents regularly brought their children to the center for these activities. The children were always very excited about engaging in activities with the seniors; however, I believe the older adults benefited even more. They treated the children as if they were their own grand children or great grand children. They gathered in small groups and with much delight read books to the children. They also told the children stories. The children listened intently and eagerly asked questions. One could see the relationships that were slowly taking shape. Other seniors joined the children as they played with brightly colored toys. This was a great way to break the ice and get the children to interact with them. The exchange between seniors and children was remarkable as the generations connected. For about an hour the seniors seemed to get lost in the children's world.

The expressions on the faces of the seniors were an indication of the joy and satisfaction they got from the experience. The activities served as a source of emotional support for these older adults. A client once shared with me that the activities took away her boredom and helped enrich her life. Indeed, intergenerational activities can rejuvenate a sense of purpose as well as increase self-esteem, stimulate learning, and improve the health of an older person. The opportunity to socialize no doubt helped them feel like productive and contributing members of society.

THE VISIT

This reminds me of the time when I took my children to visit the senior center. This was the visit that I had promised the seniors. My son was about six months old and my daughter was almost a year and a half. During our trip to the center, my son fell asleep. I thought he would be awake by the time we arrived at the center, but this was not the case. We had barely strolled into the lobby when a group of older women saw us. Immediately they approached us and their attention quickly turned to the young ones.

Realizing that my son was still asleep, the ladies began speaking in hushed tones. They gasped "oohs" and "aahs" as they admired the sleeping child. His sister even tried to get him to open his eyes, but she did not have any luck. Not getting any action from my son, they turned to my daughter.

"What's your name, little one?" one of the ladies asked. My daughter popped her head up and recited her name with a smile.

"Do you help mommy take care of your little brother?" another senior asked. My daughter responded with an emphatic nod.

"You have beautiful dimples just like your mother," another one remarked as she gently touched my daughter on the head. My daughter smiled again.

The seniors wanted to know my son's name and age. I chatted with them for a short while and then we began inching our way from the lobby to different areas of the center. The faces of the seniors lit up as they saw the children and I could hear them whispering in admiration as we moved away from them. We stayed at the center for about an hour and when we left, the seniors waved goodbye. This brief interaction may appear insignificant; however, for those seniors, just the sight of the young children brightened their day and eventually led them to start conversations about their grand children, great grand children, and even the neighbors' children. For many of them, it was obvious that family meant the world to them.

My son missed his moment in the spotlight. He woke up as we got into the car for the trip home. I told him of the many friends he had made and how he remained asleep throughout his entire visit. He gave me a half a smile while kicking his legs, as if to say "I know." Four years later, when the children visited the center, they were both able to have a conversation with the seniors. You bet a few of them reminded my son about how he slept through his first visit. This drew a round of laughter.

"A man practices the art of adventure when he breaks the chain of routine and renews his life through reading new books, traveling to new places, making new friends, taking up new hobbies and adopting new viewpoints."
— Wilfred Peterson

The Mobility Factor

Many of the seniors who attended the center took advantage of the transportation service because they had no other means of getting there. Access to transportation remains a critical issue for older adults today. The ability to get around independently means a lot to most of them. It allows them to feel fulfilled and to remain independent and active in their community. This explains in large part, the reason seniors are driving longer these days and in larger numbers. If there is any doubt that this is true, the next time you are out driving, sneak a peek at the occupants of the vehicles around you. As a Florida resident, I have noticed that thousands of retirees have made the Sunshine State their home and they are driving in large numbers.

Aging brings physical changes that can cause a person's driving skills to decline over time. By learning ways to adapt to such changes, individuals are able to continue driving. Eventually, they may have to give up driving altogether. Many older adults are insistent on driving for as long as they can. I can't say I blame them.

Their desperate need to remain mobile is paramount to their well-being. Seniors cherish the freedom of getting into their personal automobiles in order to access medical, social, religious, recreational, employment, and other services. The thought of not having this privilege is paralyzing for most and I believe that this mindset drives them to hold on tighter and longer to their car keys. Without a personal automobile, they have to seek alternate forms of transportation, which often times is not very easy. I have noticed that the number of older persons, including, the ones who attend the center, are making frequent trips to various destinations and the distance traveled is on the increase.

The decision to stop driving is never an easy one and is largely attributed to physical impairments. While a driver's license is regarded as a symbol of independence, many states have started to limit the rights of older adults who can drive. It is important to realize that the decision to stop driving or being forced to stop driving does not necessarily mean the loss of independence. The seniors who took advantage of the service provided by the center gave themselves a chance at independence when it comes to mobility. Not only did they have a ride to the senior center, they used the same service to access other destinations—free of charge. Additionally, the availability of other forms of transportation services makes the transition for them, as well as others, a little easier.

It is therefore safe to say that no single solution can resolve all of the transportation needs of the aging population in the United States. Rather, it requires a family of transportation alternatives. The most popular choices for older adults include the following:

Senior Center Transit Service – Provides free trips to seniors attending adult day programs. A simple telephone or in-person client intake generally gets seniors into the program. It is a shared-ride door-to-door or curb-to-curb system that runs on a schedule established by the different programs. Seniors are informed of their pick up or drop off times, and they receive personalized assistance and can use the same service to access other destinations.

Americans with Disabilities Act (ADA) Paratransit Service — A door-to-door transportation service available for persons with disabilities who are incapable of using the fixed-route bus service. Individuals enjoy trips to medical and recreational facilities, places of employment, shopping centers, churches and synagogues, and other locations in their community. The trips are provided in lift-equipped vehicles. The application process and eligibility requirements for this specialized service typically vary from state to state and trips are usually done in groups. Trip costs and payment arrangement also vary from system to system.

Community Bus Service — Offered in many communities and appeals to the more adventurous seniors who want to take short trips on their own. It is easier to navigate and serves routes that are not primary thoroughfares in one's community. This shuttle type service generally connects with the county-run fixed-route service and is free in some areas.

Fixed Route Bus Service — Buses travel along fixed routes with established schedules and designated stops along established routes. While there is a fare to travel on public transit systems, most services offer discounted fares for seniors. The vehicles used are wheelchair accessible, making travel by bus a good, safe, and low-cost option for older persons. Some take advantage of the travel training programs that are available for those who may feel uncomfortable using the service at first.

Family and Friends — More and more, older adults are counting on ridesharing with friends, neighbors, or family members to meet their transportation needs. A few of the seniors attending the center were transported by family members while others came with their friends. This arrangement was convenient for the seniors as they were able to come and go as they wished. Other seniors used free or low-cost transportation service provided through their church or other volunteer organizations within their community. Being aware of available community resources in advance gives senior citizens an advantage when they are in need of the service.

LICENSED TO DRIVE

It is certain that the freedom to move about easily and safely helps the elderly maintain a sense of independence and dignity. Several years ago when my parents finally decided to take up residence in South Florida, they had to confront a big challenge—transportation!

My father does not drive and my mother was not accustomed to driving in the United States. While chatting with her one day, she told me that she was preparing to attend driving school. She surprised me. She said that she did not want to burden me, or anyone else for that matter, with transporting her and her husband. After all, at the time, she was a young fifty-something who wanted to remain mobile and nothing was going to stop her. I was proud to hear of her decision and offered my support. Within days, my mother had selected a driving school and was soon engaged in driving lessons. She was proud of herself and expressed her excitement about the whole experience. She successfully completed her driving course.

This was one of the best decisions she has ever made—a decision that has significantly impacted her lifestyle, as well as her husband's. As expected, the first few days driving solo was a bit intimidating, but my mother is the fearless type. Not long afterwards, she was whizzing along the streets of South Florida. What courage!

BIKING FATHER

My father, on the contrary, is satisfied with being chauffeured around town or riding his bike in the neighborhood. About a year ago, I was sitting in the dentist's chair, waiting for a routine cleaning. My dental hygienist and I were engaged in conversation and I happened to look outside and saw a man riding slowly through the parking lot. As the windows of the dental office were quite narrow, I only had about three seconds to identify the person who was pedaling along. Right away, I recognized the person as my dad and immediately interrupted my dental hygienist to inform her. We both laughed. She was so surprised and inquired whether or not I was certain. I assured her that it was my father. He enjoys riding his bike to places close to home. Later that evening, I called and told my dad that I had seen him riding earlier. With a light chuckle, he told me that occasionally, he uses the parking lot as a shortcut.

SCARED COUPLE

One cool April afternoon, I was traveling south on the I-270 corridor in Rockville, Maryland where my family and I once lived before moving to South Florida. The traffic at that time of day was unusually light. I was driving in the far right lane and was nearing my exit when I noticed a Lincoln Towncar gliding in the lane beside me. As the car got slightly ahead of my car, it suddenly moved in front of my vehicle without warning. It was a close call. I was annoyed at the driver's action.

"What in the world is wrong with this person?" I wondered.

As swiftly as I could, I slammed on my brakes and honked my horn almost simultaneously. The car quickly made its way back into its lane and reduced its speed. As I passed by the vehicle, I swung my head toward the occupants, my face registering my anger. Suddenly my eyes made contact with those of an older couple and I quickly realized that they were visibly shaken by what had just happened.

Almost immediately I swung my head back toward the road faster than I did toward the car. In that instance, I felt ashamed and disappointed in myself. My impatience had got the better of me and the thought of two frightened elderly persons on the busy freeway scared me.

By this time, I had already exited the highway, but a quick glance in the rearview mirror revealed that the Lincoln Towncar had also exited. It occurred to me then that the couple might have been preparing to exit when they pulled in front of my car.

Still embarrassed, I made sure that the car never caught up to my vehicle at the light.

As I reflected on their misjudgment and my impatience, I realized that this could happen to anyone including me. This truly was a lesson learned. From that afternoon on I made a personal commitment to exercise care on the road, to respond defensively and responsibly under undesirable circumstances, and above all to be patient and calm.

THE EXIT

Allow me to share yet another experience that taught me to be more alert while driving. One evening as I was traveling home on the Beltway in Maryland, I drifted into the path of another vehicle. Realizing my error, I quickly swung the car back into its lane and attempted to wave an apology to the other driver. What I considered to be a kind gesture clearly did not impress him and he proceeded to teach me a lesson—at least he attempted to teach me a lesson. When I committed the unforgiving act, he laid on his car horn for several seconds. That must not have been satisfactory because he then tried deliberately to run me off the road.

I glanced through the rearview mirror, just in time to see his car approaching mine and getting dangerously close. My heart skipped a beat. To confirm that I was his target I changed lanes. I noticed he changed lanes as well. I wished at that moment there were more vehicles around; perhaps I could take cover easier. The lane change game went on for about a minute.

"What an idiot," I murmured.

I felt like I was in a scene straight out of an action movie. I kept a steady pace—not speeding. Heart pounding, I contemplated my next move; I had to come up with a game plan soon. Should I slow down or take the next exit?

Knowing that I was nearing an exit, I chose the latter. Well not exactly; I did not have a choice. My tormentor edged over toward my car and practically forced me out of the lane. I had to exit. As I did so, I glanced through the rearview mirror one more time. I was relieved to see that I was no longer being pursued. I breathed a sigh of relief!

I hope you feel better now, I thought to myself.

I slowly made my way home and spent the rest of my afternoon reflecting on the unpleasant experience and wondering what the alternative might have been. Thank goodness the exit provided an escape route. As you read this, I hope you never experience such a scare.

In retrospect, these experiences have prepared me for many eventful driving experiences in South Florida. Living and working in communities composed of large concentrations of older adults, increases the challenge of navigating the road. However, let me quickly add that this reality does not necessarily make driving any more dangerous as some would want to believe. It simply under-scores the need for all drivers to conduct them-selves responsibly.

The ability to drive and to move from place to place independently is a privilege drivers of all ages would like to maintain for as long as possible. Think for a moment about what your circumstance might be in your later years. I trust that my story will motivate you to drive carefully and defensively, and to exercise sensitivity and courtesy whenever you are behind the wheel.

MANAGING TRANSIT

Having had the responsibility of directing a local transportation system, I saw firsthand how much of a disadvantage it is not to be mobile. The elderly who cannot drive, or who are no longer able to drive, face many challenges. They must rely on other alter-natives such as the ones discussed earlier. For some, the only option is walking, which is not always safe. Not being able to move about as they wish, means that seniors must plan their trips way in advance or rely on someone else to plan their trips for them.

While mass transit and community bus service play a vital role in keeping people mobile, I learned from working at the senior center that older adults tend to prefer the smaller, seemingly less intimidating, and more personal services that are provided by their local communities. For some, accessing public transportation means walking to a bus stop. It may involve one or two connections just to get to their destination. Some trips turn into an all-day affair and often times this can be an exhausting experience for older adults. They sometimes spend hours waiting on their ride—a test of anyone's patience.

This reminds me of a time when an elderly client was waiting for a service provider to pick her up from the center. She was fine until the scheduled pick up time had passed. When she visited my office to complain, I assisted her with contacting her service provider but was unsuccessful. She finally asked that I call a taxi for her. While I knew traveling by taxi was a viable alternative, I had some trepidation about this particular client getting in a taxi as I was unsure of how familiar she was with using the service.

She sensed my hesitation and assured me that she would be okay riding alone. When the taxi arrived I made sure to document the cab driver's name and ID number along with the company name, vehicle number, and phone number. An hour later I called the client's home. She answered the telephone and I was relieved to know that she had arrived home safely.

Some seniors who rely on family members or neighbors to get them to where they want to go have shared with me that they are not always comfortable with this arrangement. They feel at times that they are being a bother and that they are interrupting the lives of other people, regardless of whether or not they are family members. Some seniors have told me that they prefer to depend on public transportation service than to rely on anyone else. They want to accomplish certain tasks on their own.

The senior center participants had the opportunity to reserve free rides to various locations such as medical facilities, grocery stores, pharmacies, banks, post offices and elsewhere. Still they must exercise responsibility in planning their trips. They must request service in a timely manner, and they must comply with certain constraints such as days and times. Often I felt their frustration as they attempted to make travel arrangements, and especially when they requested a time or date that was not available. I recall having several conversations similar to the one I am about to share with you.

THE PHONE CALL

As I sat in my office one afternoon, the telephone rang. I am not sure why I had received the call, but I decided to help. No sooner had I greeted the caller when she asked sternly, "Who am I speaking to?"

I never liked when anyone asks me that question, especially if I had already included my name in the greeting. Nonetheless, being aware of the population that I was serving, I said my name cheerfully and asked, "How may I help you?"

"Yes, I'd like a ride to my appointment on Thursday. Can you take me?"

Is the appointment for this Thursday?" I asked, mentioning the date.

"Yes, Thursday at 10:30 in the morning. I'm going for some tests," the anxious caller responded. Combing the appointment screen, I realized that the system was booked for that time. I braced myself as I prepared to tell the caller that the system could not accommodate her appointment.

In a most apologetic tone, I started informing the caller that the time slot was unavailable, but before I even had a chance to offer an alternative, she swung her proverbial bat at me.

"You can't take me?" she snapped. "I waited four weeks to get this appointment—four weeks, and now you're telling me you can't take me? What do you expect me to do now, eh? Exactly what do you want me to do now?"

Her voice sounded accusatory and she wasn't finished ranting. "Here I am, 78 years old and I've lived in this city almost all my life. I pay my taxes and you're telling me you can't get me to the doctor?" "What is wrong with you people?"

I felt trapped. I tried to get a word in, but the elderly caller muscled out my response with another volley of words.

"You know, the same thing happened to my neighbor the other day. What are you people doing over there? What did you say your name was?"

I hesitated and then repeated my name in a respectful tone.

"How do you spell that?" the caller demanded emphatically.

Slowly, I articulated the letters of my name.

At that moment, the voice quieted and I managed to offer an apology for the inconvenience, adding that we serve a large segment of the community and often the trip slots are booked very quickly, especially for morning appointments.

"Perhaps you can reschedule your appointment for a later time on the same day or for a different day," I offered.

Before she could respond, I advised, "Why don't you call your doctor's office again and see what they can do for you, and then call us back right away?"

I braced myself for her response; however, the voice of the caller had somewhat softened by this time. Maybe she was exhausted from yelling and screaming. I waited.

"Okay, I'm gonna try that, but you'd better not tell me you can't take me when I call back," she said in a half threatening, half joking tone.

I chuckled.

"Okay, ma'am, I hope we'll be able to assist you," I said assuredly. "Have a good day!"

"Okay," she replied and hung up the phone.

At that point I could only hope that we could accommodate her the next time she called.

As I reflected on that exchange, I was tempted to think that, initially, the caller was awfully rude and demanding. After all, our resources were limited and we could only serve so many people. On second thought, I imagined what would happen if the tables were turned and if I were the caller on the other end. Would my response be similar or would I have been less impatient?

I am not so sure that I can respond to that question. Access to transportation does not pose a problem for me at this time. I can get into my personal automobile at any time and drive to any place I wish. I am not burdened with having to depend on others to take me places. Hence, like some of you reading this book, I tend not to dwell on this issue. However, I have had to drastically change my perspective on this subject, having been exposed to the challenges that the elderly experience daily. I'd like to share one of these experiences with you.

The Missing Car

I am reminded of the time when I had to take my car to the shop for repairs. My husband had given me a ride to work that morning and the plan was for him to give me a ride to the shop at the end of the day so I could retrieve my vehicle. Close to my lunch break, I decided I would run some errands during that hour. I did this regularly. I gathered my handbag and cell phone and walked out to the parking area where I usually parked my car.

For a moment I stood frozen. My car was nowhere to be found! I blinked and for a few seconds my eyes swept across the parking lot when I realized that my car was really not there. I got nervous. *Who could have stolen my car?* I wondered. Then I remembered the arrangement with my husband and immediately I breathed a sigh of relief. I looked around as I composed myself, hoping no one had seen me and guessed my dilemma.

I was slightly annoyed as I made my way back to my office. My plan was ruined. I was so disappointed about not being able to do as I wished!

If only I had my car, I thought.

Then I put the experience into perspective. In fact, I felt embarrassed about how I'd reacted. The errands that I had planned on running could easily be rescheduled. At least I knew that I would have my car back at the end of the day. This is not the case with the elderly. For them, getting to the doctor, grocery stores, or pharmacy is of paramount importance. The inability of some to avail themselves of transportation service is indeed a critical matter. I have to realize that, for most seniors, their frustration comes from having to make the transition from being independent to having to rely on others for assistance.

This may sound unpopular, but planning for transportation service after giving up driving should command as much importance as planning for retirement. Many of us do not make this consideration a priority, but it is one that deserves great attention. Older adults who still drive should start addressing the issue now and not later. A self assessment of driving skills could be a first start at detecting any problems, and seeking help if needed. Family members and close friends can also be an excellent source of support to their loved ones.

Since age alone does not determine driving ability, it is hardly ever a welcome change. Family members should watch for any warning signs that may indicate a need for their loved ones to reduce driving activities or stop driving completely. This is a sensitive subject and one that should be treated with care. Family members should provide their elderly relatives with loving guidance as they help them prepare for such a lifestyle change. Having such a support can make a big difference.

Healthy Choices

The population of the United States is aging rapidly. According to the National Association of Area Agencies on Aging, in less than 25 years, the number of Americans aged 65 and older will increase to more than 71 million older Americans, which would comprise about 20 percent of the population of the United States. These are astounding numbers! It is essential therefore, for us to increase our focus on the promotion and preservation of the health of older adults, in order to effectively manage the health and economic challenges of an aging society.

Too often we hear about older adults who are unable to conduct the functions of daily living due to their declining health. All of us have seen where the lack of regular physical activity has led to serious health problems including high blood pressure, depression, obesity, and diabetes, and ultimately the reduction of the quality and length of life for older adults.

Nowadays, things are changing—for good. Significant improvements in medicine, public health, science, and technology have resulted in older Americans living longer and healthier lives than generations past. It seems that now more than ever before, more and more seniors are taking an interest in maintaining good health. Older adults want to remain healthy and independent in their homes and communities. They are beginning to realize that it is never too late to start making small lifestyle changes, which will allow them to feel better and live healthier. The experts tell us that even ten minutes of physical activity a day can impact one's health. Being physically active contributes considerably to healthy aging. A step toward a healthier lifestyle is always a winning choice! Some of the benefits the elderly can reap are:

- Reduced anxiety and depression

- Lower blood pressure

- Lower mortality rate

- Increased mental functioning

- Enhanced immune system functioning

In addition to visiting their health care provider regularly, older adults are taking advantage of health and wellness programs, health fairs, health seminars and workshops, safety programs, and health screenings. They are becoming increasingly aware of issues related to their health and are taking advantage of such programs at senior centers throughout the country.

It is no surprise these days to see seniors running marathons. They are keeping up with the forty-somethings and finishing strong as well. One other trend is seniors visiting the gyms in record numbers. The next time you visit the gym, look around the facility and you will confirm what I am talking about. Most are also taking advantage of fitness programs offered through their health insurance and that are geared strictly toward the health and wellness of the older population.

In an earlier chapter, I mentioned that my dad is fond of riding his bike around the neighborhood. My mother and I had cautioned him, even before his retirement, that he should take advantage of the wellness program that their insurance offers. This would get him out of their condo from time to time and help keep him active. He agreed, but I noticed that following his retirement, he was not making much effort to get things done. After a few conversations and much encouragement, he agreed to register in the program.

I transported him to the gym and when we arrived for our scheduled tour, a friendly member of staff welcomed us. He handed my dad an activity schedule and brochures, and proceeded to describe the activities as we looked around. When my dad saw the rows of state-of-the-art exercise equipment, his eyes lit up. Seeing his eagerness, the assistant invited him to test a piece of the equipment. Without hesitation, my father jumped on a pec deck machine and tested it for a few seconds. He loved it!

With encouragement and some guidance from the staff member, my dad carefully tested several pieces of the equipment. He was like a kid in a candy store. I had to advise him to slow down a couple times. The assistant assured me that help would be available whenever he came to exercise and he documented the equipment that seemed to be of interest to my father. We left the facility on a high note. I knew my dad could not wait until the next day to return to the gym. Since then, he has been riding his bike to the gym at least three times per week.

All of this is encouraging news since so many health conditions affect the elderly. By engaging in physical activities, older adults are strengthening their bones and muscles, controlling their blood pressure, while keeping their heart and lungs healthy. One critical service that senior centers provide its members is a program of physical fitness and wellness activities. Many seniors recognize the value of such exercise programs, which include:

- Walking

- Running

- Swimming

- Water Aerobics

- Low-impact Aerobics

- Yoga

- Tai Chi

- Jazzercise

- Chair Exercise

- Free Weights

- Fitness Machines

- And more!

Many of these options were available to the seniors where I worked and their participation was a strong indication of their awareness of the benefits of maintaining a healthier lifestyle. It is their key to maintaining healthy and independent lives. Take, for instance, the Jazzercise classes. I noticed that the Jazzercise classes attracted many more senior participants than any other activity at the center. The classes were always at capacity with several names on a wait list. This total-body conditioning program combines the art of jazz dance and the beat of popular music. There was no mistaking when Jazzercise was in session. The upbeat tempo of the music filled the large gym and bounced off its mirror-lined walls into nearby rooms. Even with the doors closed the sound could not be contained. Such, too, was the enthusiasm of the participants.

A peek inside the gymnasium revealed regularly practiced routines. It was clear that Jazzercise was not for the faint of heart. Some seemed tired, but none appeared to want to take a break. Their facial expression spelled determination and at the end of the session, one could easily assume the effort was worth it. Following each session, participants gathered in small groups to talk about their experience. It was as if they had just left the stage after a dazzling performance in front of an enthusiastic house.

One member of the group who had never missed a practice told me that she enjoyed the activity greatly. She said that the exercise helped her stay healthy and she enjoyed the relationships she had developed with members of the group.

"Nothing will ever stand between me and my Jazzercise," she admitted with a giggle.

Her friend chimed in, "Ditto, ditto!"

They both admitted that Jazzercise helps them relieve stress, plus they want to "look and feel good."

Another attention getter at the senior center was Tai Chi. This Chinese form of slow, physical exercise attracted even the younger seniors. Tai Chi helps improve a person's balance and lessens the chances of falling—a frequent occurrence among seniors. Like Jazzercise, there was never a problem filling Tai Chi classes at the senior center. People generally practice Tai Chi for various reasons. However, it was clear to me that these seniors were in it for their physical, mental, and social well-being. The moves they practiced involved weight-bearing and non-weight-bearing stances, proper alignment of their bodies, and repeated, coordinated movements that they did in a continuous and circular manner. It was not easy for some of them, but they hung in there and did the best they could. They seemed to like the effect the exercise had on them and they kept coming back.

Likewise, the water aerobics program was a huge draw. Tucked away in the back of the facility was a three feet deep therapeutic pool. Its blue water stood glistening under the Florida sun. Before anyone created a ripple, it painted a picture of beauty and serenity. I noticed repeatedly that the pool always seemed to capture the attention of those seeing it for the first time.

"How deep is it?" they would ask.

"Can anyone use it or do you need special permission?"

The seniors who used the pool amenities found it refreshing and exhilarating. Studies have shown that aerobic exercise can boost the aging mind and body. The seniors who did water aerobics must have realized its benefits as they regularly participated in the activity. Some swam alone or with their friends, while others did group exercises. What was equally encouraging were the provisions made for those who used mobility devices, such as wheelchairs. Everyone was accommodated; no one was excluded. Hence, there was no reason not to experience the benefits. While some seniors did not enter the pool, they enjoyed themselves stretched out at poolside soaking up the warm Florida sunshine. With the availability of ample supervision by staff, everyone felt safe hanging out in and around the pool.

IN WALKING DISTANCE

About ten years ago, I was sitting with a group of professionals preparing to leave for a trip from a local mall. It was a few minutes before eight o'clock, long before the stores were open. As I entered the mall, I noticed several older adults walking around.

At first I was perplexed. Never having gone to a mall that early in the day, I thought these people were mighty anxious to shop. As I looked around, however, I noticed that there were more seniors taking long strides and walking briskly. Then I managed to spot what seemed like dumbbells. A closer look at what these individuals were holding confirmed that they were carrying brightly colored dumbbells, which might have weighed about ten pounds. It was at that moment that I realized the intentions of these seniors were far from shopping—at least at that moment. They were there to exercise. What a fantastic idea!

I remember standing for a while watching these individuals with simple admiration for being health-conscious. Here they were, in a cool and safe environment, walking up and down the aisles of the mall with little, if any, distractions. I doubt they noticed my curiosity.

In that instant, it occurred to me that I have only regarded the mall as merely a place to meet friends, shop, eat and be entertained. Most times I end up spending too much money and I am sure that I am not alone. I also came to terms with the realization that I needed to shift my workout routine into high gear. You will agree that sometimes it takes something or someone to get us to change our perspective on any matter or provide an extra source of motivation. Seeing those seniors walk, and with such determination, was all the motivation and inspiration I needed that day. Who would have thought that the mall could help one to regroup, refocus, and stay healthy?

This explains why the response is always overwhelming when senior centers offer walking trips to the mall or even to the beach. Despite the time commitment and the hard work involved, the dividends from these exercise programs are great and seniors recognize their benefits and are cashing in! To top it off, they are having buckets of fun!

Much can be said about some seniors who jog, swim, bike, ski and even hike during their later years. This is more than what some of their younger counterparts do. Our lifestyle seems to dictate the level of commitment and involvement in such activities, notwithstanding their value.

Like many, I lead a busy lifestyle, and sometimes I find it difficult to add any form of exercise program to my schedule. Ten years ago, I looked at the world around me and listened to what medical professionals and others were advising the population to do in order to stay healthy. I knew that having an exercise program of my own was not only vital, but imminent.

If you guessed that writing these lines ought to motivate me, you guessed right! Today, I have sharpened my perspective on this area of my life. I remain committed to an at-home exercise routine and have added a zumba class in between. Consistency is critical and already I am reaping the benefits. There is no question that a regular exercise program helps protect against certain health issues and enhances one's wellbeing.

DEBUNK THESE MYTHS REGARDING EXERCISE AND THE ELDERLY

Seniors should be mindful of a few myths regarding exercise and the elderly. When in doubt, it's a good idea to speak with a healthcare provider or a

family member who can guide you. Be on the alert
for these myths:

Myth #1

Older adults should not waste their time exercising; they are getting old anyway.

The fact is by doing exercise and strength training, your body will look and feel younger and you will remain active longer. Reap the benefits of regular physical activity: lower risk for conditions, such as heart disease, diabetes, high blood pressure, Alzheimer's and dementia, colon cancer, and obesity.

Myth #2

Older adults should not start an exercise regimen now; it's too late and they are already old.

The fact is you're never too old to exercise! If you have not exercised in a while or you have never exercised before, you should begin your exercise regime with light walking and other activities that are not too strenuous. It is also a good idea to talk to your doctor before starting any exercise program.

Myth #3

Exercise may lead to slip, trips, and fall accidents.

The fact is you will help shore up your strength and stamina when you exercise regularly. This practice will help prevent loss of bone mass and improve your balance, which will reduce your risk of falling.

Myth #4

Elderly people should not maintain an exercise regimen; they should relax and save their energy and strength.

The fact is it is absolutely unhealthy for older adults to live a sedentary lifestyle. Inactivity can and will result in loss of the ability to do things independently and can increase reliance on medicines for illnesses and invite more hospitalizations and doctor visits.

Myth #5

The disabilities of the elderly will prevent them from exercising while sitting down.

The fact is even while seated in a wheelchair or an armchair an older person can lift light weights, stretch, and engage in chair aerobics. Such activity will improve muscle tone, increase range of motion, and enhance cardiovascular health.

POOL TIME

Compared to the other activities, the game of pool seemed not as popular, yet it attracted several males and a handful of females. I saw the same group play regularly. The pool room was large and airy. On the few occasions that I watched this group, the scene seemed similar. A few men stood in a corner having a quiet conversation. In the other corner, a small group chatted lively and loudly. Others complained about the temperature in the room—it was too cold for them. The temperature did not appear to distract the players whose eyes were fixed intently on the big green pool table with the colorful balls sitting on top. Nothing, it appeared, could break their concentration. After some posturing, long analytical steers at the balls, and even what seemed like a little dance, there was action, and the colorful balls rolled swiftly in all directions atop the big green table. This drew a joyful "Yes!" or a disappointing "Augh!" from the players. A few men, who were preparing their pool cues, paused for a moment and turned to see how the play ended. Seconds later they resumed their task as they studied the game while waiting their turn. The players were not sweating and they did not seem exhausted, but one thing was certain—they were focused! Their hand-eye coordination was in motion and their analytical senses were hard at work—a cognitive advantage.

MIND GAMES

Seniors recognize that a quality lifestyle includes attention to their intellect and emotions. With memory playing an important role in all cognitive activities, including reading, reasoning, and mental calculation, it is noticeable when these skills begin to fail. Older persons need mental stimulation and interaction in order to maintain their ability to communicate. A lifestyle with organized activities, such as the ones described earlier, provides great social opportunities for them. Mind, body, and soul must work in concert to create the balance they desire and that we all crave. Let's face it; it is a challenge for some seniors more than it is for others to become active participants. Nonetheless, even a modest level of participation goes a long way.

The older adults whom I saw at the senior center regularly immersed themselves in such activities as health education classes, lectures, health screenings, or playing a musical instrument. This explains why almost every time that I see my mother-in-law, she is working on a crossword puzzle. With a smile, she tells me, "It helps to keep my mind sharp." Good for her!

The book club, as well as organized group discussions, attracted a modest crowd. Bear in mind that these are individuals who have lived incredible lifestyles and have amassed a lifetime of experiences. They had a lot to share. Besides, the in-depth discussions brought out different viewpoints and increased their awareness and appreciation of their cultural diversity and the world around them.

Aside from the obvious benefits of exercising the mind and cultivating a positive outlook on life, these activities promoted social interaction among the seniors. They were able to exchange ideas and share their experiences and opinions, and many had a lot to divulge. Throughout the center, small pockets of seniors engaged in other games including scrabble, bridge, MahJong, or dominoes. Sometimes it brought out the best in the seniors and at other times it brought out the worst in them. It was not unusual, therefore, for a few tempers to flare occasionally during the time they spent together. There were always a few sore losers in the group. All in all, it was clear to me that the attitudes did not get in the way of the activities for too long. When seniors take advantage of such activities, it gives them an opportunity to reminisce, share life experiences, and connect with their community.

Nutrition Sense

In promoting a healthy lifestyle, another important factor that I would encourage seniors to consider is practicing good nutrition. Senior centers are making eating well a fun activity by providing nutritious meals to their participants. I recall the daily lunches served at the center. A large percentage of seniors ate at the center; however, few of them brought their own lunches. Others bought food at the gift shop. I also recall seniors participating in many nutrition classes and activities. Many of these events were hosted by on-site staff; some were hosted by visiting culinary and nutrition professionals in the aging network. They also provided counseling and risk screening. The availability of these classes and services allowed senior centers to share useful information to its members, caregivers, as well as others in the community. They learned about good eating practices, preparation of healthy meals, proper food storage practices, comparing food prices, buying items in bulk, cooking in large batches, and discovering ways to stretch their dollars. Many seniors are eating on a budget, especially in the current economy, so they welcome any guidance and assistance they receive.

Developing good eating habits and getting enough rest can be a winning combination! Many times when I walked around the center, I noticed that a few seniors were taking a nap; some were in deep sleep. If they were not napping, they were relaxing with their eyes closed. How I envied them! Research shows that napping even for 20 minutes can help refresh the mind, boost mood, improve overall alertness, and increase productivity. This, my friends, is encouraging news! Whenever I manage to squeeze in a power nap at home, I always wake up feeling revitalized and alert. Whether or not the seniors were aware of the benefits, and I believe most did, they were doing themselves a world of good.

VOLUNTEER A HUG

In chapter five of this book, I wrote about the volunteer service that the seniors offered their community. Volunteering is a healthy choice. Several studies have shown that older adults who volunteer regularly tend to be happier as a group than those who do not volunteer. Researchers have also found that volunteering may help the elderly stay healthy and may even prolong their lives. I have spoken with many older adults who shared that they volunteer their time, not only to give back to their community, but to keep themselves active and engaged. The joy and satisfaction they receive from these experiences increase their self esteem and make them feel more worthwhile. Now that's a healthy choice!

From time to time, I would notice a group of seniors walking throughout the center smiling, laughing, and giving hugs to other seniors, as well as staff members. They were a happy group and they created quite a stir whenever they stepped into action. Their sole purpose was to make someone—anyone, happy. Smiling and laughing improves one's mood and health. Laughter relieves stress and improves the immune system. It is described as an internal jog; massaging and exercising our inner organs. I bet those seniors knew that smiling is good medicine for their mood and for their health. I bet they knew that when they smiled they were exercising fourteen facial muscles; stretching their lungs, relaxing their chests, and breathing easier.

When we can laugh at something and even at ourselves, we change our perspective and our attitude. For that moment, we distract ourselves from our problems and, maybe, from our physical discomforts. Life appears to get better when we laugh. Did you realize that as your mood improves, you open yourself to new possibilities? Other people, noticing the change, respond differently to you and soon you may be laughing and smiling as well. Smile on purpose, even if you don't feel like it! Go ahead, give it a try!

Similarly, hugging has its benefits! Hugging is described as a miracle medicine that can relieve many physical and emotional problems. Its benefits include helping you live longer, protecting against illness, curing depression and stress, and strengthening family relationships. Research shows that when a person is touched, it significantly increases the amount of hemoglobin in their blood, which in turn tones up the body, speeds up recovery from illness, and fights against diseases. I'm sure the act of hugging had similar effects on those seniors who shared a hug with someone. A hug, a smile, or making someone laugh is a simple act of kindness that all of us can share.

A MOMENT OF INTIMACY

The need for intimacy is ageless. Do not think for a moment that our need for closeness and intimacy diminishes as the years go by. Realize that as a person gets older and his or her health declines, more and more, that person will need someone to reach out to them. The kind and loving touch of family members, friends, caregivers and acquaintances is crucial in the lives of those who might not be able to physically reach out and express their love.

Direct intimacy is also important. We welcome a warm hug and holding the hand of someone we care about. Surely, such factors as the loss of a loved one, use of drugs, disorders, or lack of privacy can get in the way of the elderly developing and maintaining such relationships or at least change the way in which they express their love and friendship of those they care about.

Nonetheless, a healthy sexual relationship can positively affect all aspects of an older adult's life, including physical health and self-esteem. This includes enjoying sex and intimate relationships. A 2009 survey about sexual attitudes and practices of 1,670 adults ages 45 and older conducted by the AARP, found that sexual health is an essential element of the quality of life of middle aged and older adults. The research found that healthy and physically active survey respondents were generally more satisfied with their sex lives than those who were not.

I cannot say to what extent the older adults at the senior center were enjoying sex and intimate relationships. However, there were several married couples among the membership and it was evident that some single males and females were looking for love. Some had just lost a spouse and were trying to rebound. While others were not seeking to get involved in an intimate relationship, they craved the companionship of someone of the opposite sex. I recall one such couple, who became fast friends and it was not too long afterwards that they were being referred to as a "hot item." I wanted to see for myself, so I posted up by the entrance of the center one afternoon and sure enough, there they were, arm in arm walking through the lobby and sporting big smiles.

He was about six feet tall and very well built. She was half his height and petite. Forget about the difference in their stature; they were a happy couple and they seemed never to separate from each other. They went on trips together, ate together, and waited on the bus together. It was as beautiful thing to watch. In case you were wondering, they did find time to share with other seniors. I am aware of at least two marriages that have resulted from these intimate relationships that developed among the members.

Yes, some seniors want to love and laugh and not be alone. They want a trusted friend in whom they can confide, share their emotions, or just have plain fun. Age does not preclude them from getting what they want out of life at this stage. By diligently working together and addressing the needs of the current generations, as well as future generations, we can ensure that every elderly person has the opportunity to make the choices that will allow them to live and enjoy a healthy and rewarding lifestyle. Starting today, think of how you can contribute to the health of an older person. It is easier than you think. Begin with offering a smile, a hug, or a greeting the next time you come in contact with an older person and you, too, will reap the benefits.

It is my hope that each of us, young or old, recognizes that this type of engagement brings a sense of balance and fulfillment to our lives, while affecting our overall well-being in a positive way.

The purpose of life, after all, is to live it, to taste experience to the utmost, to reach out eagerly and without fear for newer and richer experience.
— Eleanor Roosevelt

Staying Put

I wish more seniors would have an opportunity to age for as long as they can, in an environment in which they are familiar and that supports their healthy lifestyles. Aging should be experienced wherever the elderly call home. Over the last fifty years, many seniors have benefited from new developments in health care, economic security, and myriad of services available in their communities.

Everyday local government agencies make decisions that affect the degree to which seniors can age in place. The sooner these agencies recognize the impact that an aging population will have on a community, the better they will be at making decisions and implementing changes that will serve a maturing population well. Some cities and counties are already ramping up their efforts to put in place "age-friendly" communities that cater to the varying and changing needs of seniors. A few key strategies that may help support "age-friendly" communities are aging services networks, community partnership and collaborations, and resources that can be brought to the aging population.

Baby boomers are already playing a role in the development of such communities because they see the potential value; some have experienced it. They want to stay in touch with their social networks wherever they are and have easy access to basic health care. They welcome community services as well as the opportunity for lifelong learning. This explains their participation in the book clubs, computer classes, and other forums available at the senior center. Seniors are also taking advantage of non-degree courses offered at local universities and colleges. The purpose for having such a community structure is to optimize the social, emotional, mental, and spiritual wellbeing, as well as independence among residents. In other words, the community structure must support and enhance the quality of life of every person.

If indeed, the amenities mentioned are made a staple in our communities, fewer seniors with the support of their caregivers would rely on moving to nursing homes and assisted living facilities. Institutionalization of the elderly does not have to be a first choice, if a choice at all. Nonetheless, it is a decision with which many families grapple. It can be difficult and stressful for family members and traumatic for the older person as well.

It does not have to be so burdensome if the appropriate preparation is made. Older adults and their families should arm themselves with information about the resources that are available in their communities. When local governments, in collaboration with local businesses, provide services for seniors to age in place, they give seniors and their caregivers the confidence to delay or postpone moving seniors from the place with which they are most familiar—home.

I often reflect on the time spent with my grandparents. In retrospect, I wish I had spent more time with them. My maternal grandmother, Ancella, passed away in March 2011. I grew up calling her Aunt Annie. I still do not know how that came about, but the name stuck. As a child, I remember spending time with her. She had a kind heart and was never short on sound advice and instructions. Before she passed away, we lived miles apart, and I seldom got to see her. She was only a phone call away, however, and even though her hearing impairment made it difficult to communicate with her on the phone, that was our only means of communication. I wrote letters, but in this age of technology, I must admit that I did not write very often. During every phone conversation, she always asked me, "When next will I see you?" The question still rings in my ear. I felt guilty every time I told her that I would see her soon.

"Soon" finally came and Aunt Annie's prayers were answered in June 2010, when my family and I took a short trip to the beautiful island of Jamaica where I had an opportunity to visit my grandmother. My mother had placed her in a nursing home only a week earlier. She had lived a full life and was always surrounded by family members. My parents also made annual visits to see her.

As soon as my mother noticed her physical decline, she arranged for Aunt Annie's sister, Violet, to be her caregiver. When Violet was no longer capable of caring for Aunt Annie, my mother's only option was to place Aunt Annie in a nursing home. My mother wanted to make sure that her mom would be well cared for and that she would be safe in her absence. By all accounts, she was well cared for.

With the onset of dementia, I worried that my grandmother might not recognize us when my family and I visited her. I was so wrong. It took her only a few seconds to know who we were. She hugged and kissed each of us, all the while uttering terms of endearment. She still had her infectious smile and laughter, and she chatted and laughed a lot during the entire visit. While she repeated a few words and phrases and confused our names sometimes, she remembered our faces. Our reunion was bitter sweet.

Upon our departure, as I hugged and kissed my grandmother, I wished that she could have accompanied us back to the United States. Her circumstances did not allow her to travel. My only consolation was that she was in a comfortable and safe environment and better yet, the staff at the home informed us that she got the most visitors. Her friends and other relatives visited her regularly. I felt better on hearing that news. The home had a small population and a professional staff who really took excellent care of its residents. Still, I left my grandmother with tears in my eyes.

As more seniors have an opportunity to remain longer in their homes, the need for caregiver resources and support will increase. This is the time when the elderly will seek assistance with various tasks, such as:

- Personal and physical care

- Shopping

- Driving

- Special needs

- Household and outdoor chores

- Legal and financial matters

- And more!

They need to seek help from people on whom they can depend and trust. Adult children and spouses represent a large percentage of family caregivers. They provide these services out of love, respect, and commitment for their loved ones. The elderly also rely on friends, neighbors, and church members. Those who can afford it, employ help.

Especially with the increasing incidents of fraud and abuse against the elderly, extra care is needed to ensure the safety and wellbeing of the elderly. A high percentage of the clients who participated in the Alzheimer's program at the center had caregivers who were family members, friends or paid employees. This was a blessing. One could see the love and care with which they treated their loved ones. These caregivers also interacted warmly with the staff and supported the programs in various ways.

Sadly, some of the general population seniors with whom I came in contact needed a caregiver. It was clear that they were barely making it on their own. From dirty and tattered clothing to unkempt hair and bad breath, they were acutely in need of attention. The professionals at the senior center were very well trained to recognize such individuals and to set in motion a plan of action to assist them readily. Most of the seniors who found themselves in such predicament responded gratefully to the assistance. For others, there were no easy solutions, yet there was always a system in place to prevent their circumstances from worsening.

FINDING A HOMEMAKER/COMPANION

Seniors who are seeking a provider for homemaker or companion service should do a thorough search and enlist the help of their family when needed. Here are some options they may explore:

- A home health agency that is licensed

- A nurse registry

- An organization in the local community that has links to the Area Agency on Aging

- Individual homemakers and companions who may not be registered with a state agency and who work independently

Seniors should seek answers to important questions, such as: How long has the business been in operation? What are its hiring and training protocols? Is the agency a member of the Better Business Bureau or local Chamber of Commerce? Is the agency licensed, bonded, and ensured? What is its billing schedule? Seniors should ask for letters of recommendation as well. The time dedicated to doing quality research before making a decision might save much headache later.

WAYS TO AVOID CAREGIVER BURNOUT

If you are one of the millions of people who are caring for their parents while juggling the responsibilities of home and children, it is important that you take the necessary steps to ensure your own health. Attending to your own needs will help you be a better caregiver. Here are a few warning signs to heed as well as steps you can take to lighten the load:

- Heed these warning signs: reduced social interactions, lack of energy, feelings of pessimism, increase in alcohol use or medication to relax

- Find a caregiver support group in your community (senior centers generally host support groups)

- Seek help from a family member, friend, or someone in whom you can confide

- Seek respite care from one of the agencies mentioned under the "Finding a Homemaker/Companion" section of this book

- Establish reasonable limits—know when too much is too much

- Practice healthy lifestyle habits—eat a variety of foods, exercise regularly, get adequate sleep each day

- Dispensing care from a state of physical, emotional, and spiritual stability will result in better relations with those for whom we care, and in the end, all parties benefit. This strategy might not come easily for some, but it's an effort that is worthwhile pursuing on purpose.

I do not want to get to the end of my life and find that I just lived the length of it. I want to have lived the width of it as well.
-Diane Ackerman

Paying Respect

Paying respect to the elderly should begin at a very early age. Each of us has an opportunity to develop our own way of paying respect to the elderly, starting with those who are closest to us. Whether we offer a gift, help with a task, spend time in conversation, share a meal, or give a smile or hug, we can make a difference in the life of an older person. Our actions will lead to a culture of honor and respect for the elderly.

As a nation, we can do more to honor and respect older adults, many of whom have made positive contributions to our society. Their many accomplishments are great and it is our responsibility to work at improving our communities so that the elderly among us may prosper independently and with dignity.

The values that my parents taught me have served me well. Respect, love, honesty, integrity, diligence, and perseverance are values that I incorporate daily in my life. Growing up in the Caribbean, I was instructed to be respectful to my elders in particular. I was expected to offer a greeting or listen attentively when I was being addressed by an older person. Likewise, I was expected to grant assistance when reasonably possible. It was my duty and it was best that I did not step out of line or else my parents would have reminded me in no uncertain terms. I am glad for that. Consequently, respecting the elderly is a given for me. They are our mothers, fathers, sisters, brothers, aunts, uncles, cousins, friends, and acquaintances. They are family!

The elderly have experienced good times and bad, many have been successful, others have not been so successful, but they have contributed to society in varying ways. They have laughed and cried. They have loved and have been ignored. They have nurtured and have been denied nurturing. They have been doctors, attorneys, professors, preachers, painters, actors, storytellers, farmers, seamstresses, writers, artists, and so much more. They have been our role models!

The elderly possess a wealth of valuable information and most of them are willing to share, if only we would engage them. Their years of experience can drive the success and survival of generations to come. It is therefore important to me, as it should be to everyone, to hold them in high esteem. We must honor them and acknowledge their presence among us.

In 1963, President John F. Kennedy convened a meeting with the National Council of Senior Citizens to address increasing concerns over the elder population. Almost a third had survived poverty and had received little help in meeting their increasing needs. That year, the President designated May as Senior Citizens Month. Seventeen years later, President Jimmy Carter changed the name to Older Americans Month. Since that time, every American President has issued a formal proclamation asking for citizens to honor older Americans.

Our nation also celebrates National Grandparents Day annually. I wonder how many of you are aware of this fact. The first national holiday honoring grandparents was proclaimed by West Virginia's Governor, Arch Moore, in 1973. Principal among those who influenced this proclamation was Miriam McQuade, a West Virginia mother of fifteen, who used her position as a delegate to the White House Conference on Aging to drum up national attention for her cause.

Five years later, the United States Congress passed legislation proclaiming the first Sunday after Labor Day as National Grandparents Day. Then President, Jimmy Carter, selected the September date to signify the "autumn years" of life. The holiday has a three-fold purpose—taking time to honor grandparents, allowing grandparents to show their love for their grandchildren, and making children aware of the strength, information, and guidance older people can offer.

Looking back, I remember how much I enjoyed the stories my grandmother told me. Some were pleasant and some were not so pleasant, as life was not always easy for her. Nonetheless, the stories intrigued me. She always offered kind advice and lavished her care and love in many ways. It was so enlightening and reassuring to share in her wisdom. This exposure has led me to contemplate my current stage in life and what my legacy will be. As I "think forward," I realize that I have the capacity to accomplish what seems impossible, while I reflect on the guidance and kind instructions of my loving grandmother.

Older persons enjoy the company of others. They like to express their thoughts and share their experiences and dreams. While some are reserved in their demeanor, others will unceremoniously invite you into their hearts and soul. This gesture can be surprisingly refreshing and downright revealing. I have learned to understand and appreciate them even more through our interactions.

Older adults are also great conversationalists. As I observed them from time to time at the center—sitting on the bench, waiting on the bus, sharing in a current events class, they are always in conversation. Some seniors may not initiate a conversation because they are waiting for someone else to invite them into their world. Once they have gotten beyond this hurdle, some will undoubtedly share their innermost thoughts and fears.

They sometimes reminisced about their childhood—good or bad. They discussed past careers and hobbies. Many proudly expressed their professional accomplishments with joy. They gloated over favorite family members who mean the world to them—sons, daughters, grand children—or express their dissatisfaction or disappointment with others. I have heard of accounts of successful and caring children and grandchildren who treated them well. I have also been told of some unpleasant occurrences and the manner in which they managed to overcome. The stories were many, varied, and captivating. The conversations left me feeling sad and empathetic or happy and hopeful.

Every so often I would take a few minutes to engage a client or two in conversation. I would catch them sitting in the lobby, eating in the gift shop, or chatting with friends in the main hall. They always welcomed me heartily. They appreciated anyone who took the time to acknowledge them. I have never been able to sit at just one table to talk with a few seniors without having to table hop. I had to make my way to two or three more tables, if it was even to say, "Hello, everyone."

Sounds simple, doesn't it? I can assure you that for an older adult, this gesture often goes a long way.

It is like an exercise—the benefits are far-reaching. Let me add that the seniors were not the sole beneficiaries in this case. It was invigorating for me to observe the smiles and gestures that were reciprocated. It was refreshing to know that such a simple act could have such a profound impact on a human being. The images of the focal point are forever etched on the canvas of my mind. Indeed, they will linger in my memory and carry me for a very long time. What happens at senior centers should not stay at senior centers. It is an opportunity for each of us to broadcast their value, while raising awareness of the importance and the need to honor and respect our elders and those we love. Who would have thought that a beautiful Florida morning when I pulled into the oddly-shaped parking lot of the senior center would end on such a high note.

> Do all the good you can to all the people you can for as long as you can!
> —Anonymous

PART II

It's Not the End of the Journey

It was a warm South Florida afternoon and Grandma Rose is visiting her daughter, Denise, and her family. Grandma Rose was ill for a couple weeks and was unable to drive. Her husband, Bobbie, doesn't drive, so it was difficult for both of them during her time of illness. Luckily, they were able to get around with the help of their daughter, friends and neighbors. Grandma Rose is feeling much better these days so she decided to go visiting!

Denise was in the middle of preparing the evening meal when she heard the chiming of the door bell. She went to get the door. She knew who the visitor was, because Grandma Rose had already called her. However, she had not told her children, Rick and Ora, that their grandmother was coming over.

Denise greeted her mother at the door with a big hug and the two made their way toward the kitchen. A burst of laughter from the women got Ora's attention. Immediately she thought of her grandmother, but she wasn't too sure. Then she

heard the voice—the distinct voice of her grandmother and she darted from her bedroom towards
the kitchen.

"Grandma, Grandma, you're here! I'm so happy
you're feeling better! Did you drive over here by
yourself?" Ora asked.

"Hey, Pumpkin, I sure did," Grandma Rose
replied as she reached out to hug her granddaugh-
ter. "It feels good to be driving again!" she exclaimed
with a broad smile. "I didn't like having to ask your
mom to drive me to my medical appointments and
to the grocery store. Whew! She has enough to
do already!"

"Where's Grandpa Bobbie?" Ora asked.

"Ah, I left him at home taking a nap," the child's grandmother responded.

"Why didn't he come?" Ora asked.

"Oh, you'll just have to ask him the next time you see him, child."

Ora sat next to her grandmother in the kitchen where Denise was almost finished preparing dinner. Just then, Grandma Rose looked outside and noticed her grandson, Rick. He was playing with his game on the back patio and had not heard the doorbell. She tapped on the window lightly to get his attention. Rick quickly looked up startled, and at the sight of his grandmother, his face lit up and he darted toward the sliding glass door and headed for the kitchen.

"Grandma, hi, Grandma, I heard you got lost the other day!" he exclaimed with a puzzled look on his face.

Grandma Rose gave him a reassuring hug and smiled.

"Oh, I just made a wrong turn, kiddo. Your grandfather was with me and between the two of us, we found our way back."

"You should get a GPS like Dad's," Rick advised.

"Yeah, Grandma," his sister chimed in. "A GPS is a great idea!"

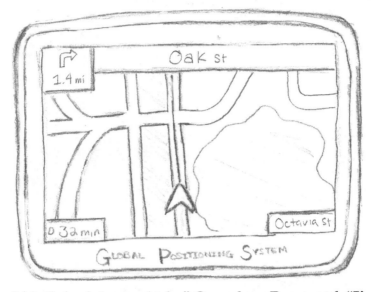

"Ah, I don't know, kids," Grandma Rose said. "I'm just not familiar with the new gadgets these days."

"Grandma, I just don't want you and Grandpa to get lost again," Rick exclaimed. "It's really easy to learn; you should try it."

For a brief moment, Grandma Rose looked away and began wondering what it would be like to no longer be able to drive. She wouldn't want to depend on her family forever nor her best friend, Daphne, to transport her, she thought. A few moments later, she once again turned her attention back to her family.

As the children chatted with their grandmother, Denise, remarked, "Mom, your grandchildren are really worried about you, aren't they? I have to say that I'm a little concerned, too."

Rose gave a weak smile and briefly turned her attention to the small bird that had suddenly perched on the rose bush by the patio.

"You know, Mom, I noticed a dent on your car last time you were here and, while there's no need for alarm, I'm just a bit concerned for your safety. "Have you thought of how you and dad will get around when you can no longer drive?"

With a look of concern, her mom responded, "You know, Denise, I don't even want to think about that now—not sure what I'd do, really."

To lighten the moment, Denise said with a chuckle, "Mom, I know you still have some driving left in you! She turned and looked at her mother. You and dad enjoy your independence, but now may be a good time to start thinking of some alternatives—what do you say?"

Noticing the look of concern on her mother's face, Denise stopped what she was doing and turned towards her.

"Mama Rose," she said jokingly, "there's life after driving!"

Rose managed to squeeze out a half a smile.

"Yes, there is," her daughter assured her, and looking directly at her children, she quickly followed up with, "the kids and I can work on some transportation options for you. What do you say?"

At that moment, Ora gave her grandmother another hug as Rick leaned his head on her shoulder and whispered, "We'll help you, Grandma, don't worry."

"Alright, alright!" Rose answered softly, with a shy grin as she looked at the children and then to her daughter. She sounded relieved. Then almost immediately, she blurted out, "But I'm not getting on any of those big, long city buses I see on the streets."

Denise laughed heartily at her mother's feisty comment.

"Mom," Denise assured her, "Don't worry. They're really not as scary as you think. There are several other ways of getting around town if you don't like the buses. Then again, you know you can get travel training to ride those buses, right?"

You're kidding me!" her mom remarked. "They have people who'll teach you how to ride the buses?"

"Yeah, I'm serious; it takes some of the fear out of the experience! You can always call a taxi, but you know that's not cheap! Of course, we'll always be here for you and dad."

"How else can we get transportation service?" Grandma Rose asked.

"Well," said Denise. "I have another idea. You and dad can use the local senior center transportation service and later on if you're eligible, you can take advantage of the ADA paratransit service that the county offers.

"What's that?" Grandma Rose asked.

"Oh, it's complementary service for people with disabilities. I don't think you two are eligible for that service right now, but you can surely use the senior center service. It's safe and convenient, and they'll come to the house to pick you up."

"Is it like having your own chauffeur?" Grandma Rose asked.

"No, no, no, Mom, it's a shared ride system; which means that in most cases there will be other people in the vehicle with you. It's like riding with a few friends. Anyway, Mom, we'll talk more about this another time. Okay? You and dad will be just fine. In the meantime, enjoy your grandchildren!"

Rose seemed relieved as her two grandchildren held her arms and led her toward their bedrooms. As the three of them walked away, Denise, announced, "I hope you plan on staying for dinner, Mom! Your son-in-law will be home by then and he and the kids can show you how the GPS works!"

Rose did not respond and as she sat in Ora's room, her mind lingered on the thought of relying on a GPS to help her get around town. It might not be a bad idea, she contemplated. Still, she was curious to know more about the senior center service. She got lost in her own thoughts until Ora slowly said, "Grandmaaa, you're not lis-tening."

Grandma Rose quickly looked up at Ora and smiled. Then she admitted that she was picturing herself riding on one of the buses Denise talked about.

"I don't want to give up driving," she said with a hint of sadness in her voice.

"Don't worry, Grandma, it will be okay," Ora assured her.

"Why don't you talk to mom about that another time?" Rick chimed in.

"You kids sure know how to make me feel better; that's why I love you so much."

With that said, the two children changed the subject to a discussion about their activities in school. Grandma Rose looked at recent photographs of the children and admired trophies, certificates, and other awards they had won. She was having a terrific time talking and laughing with the children when suddenly, there was a knock on the door, which was slightly ajar. It startled everyone. They looked up to see Derrick, the children's father smiling at them.

"Dad, you scared us!" screamed Ora.

Before the children's father could greet them, Rick yelled, "Dad, Grandma wants you to show her how to use the GPS!"

Derrick looked over at his mother-in-law and with a smile asked, "Is this true?"

She glanced at Rick and then back at Derrick and replied, "Maybe."

"Okay," Derrick said, "I believe Denise is getting ready to serve dinner, so let's eat first and then

I'll see about giving you a crash course in using my GPS."

On that note, everyone moved toward the dining room. Denise had prepared one of her family's favorite meals: fried chicken, rice and beans, macaroni and cheese, biscuits, lots of steamed vegetables, and a few extra trimmings. The family chatted happily throughout dinner.

"That meal was delicious! I'll have to take some back for Bobbie," Grandma Rose said when she was finished eating. "I'll be ready for my class in a few minutes," she said to Derrick with a smirk on her face.

Step by step, Derrick patiently explained to Grandma Rose the many features of the GPS. The challenge began when it was Grandma's turn to test the instrument. She held the device close to her face and spun it around a couple times.

"Grandma, where do you want to go?" Rick asked.

"Hmmm, home!" his grandmother said with a chuckle.

"Well, type in the instructions, Grandma!" Rick interjected.

"Okay, young man, let's see," she said.

Without hesitation, Grandma Rose began exploring and through trial and error, she started warming up to the little instrument. In fact, it was obvious that when she added her address and selected the "go" command and the map appeared, she was surprised. With a wide smile, she admitted, "It worked. That wasn't so bad."

Both children chimed in, "See?"

Denise encouraged her mother to add a few more addresses to be sure she was comfortable. Grandma Rose did and then she turned to Derrick and said, "Maybe I can use one of these things after all!"

Derrick smiled and replied, "Just let me know when you're ready, Rose, and I'll get one for you. Her gentle nod indicated that she was ready to give it a try.

Within two weeks, Grandma Rose was holding her own GPS. Denise gave her a refresher course and she seemed ready to put it to use. For several months Grandma Rose used her GPS on and off. Every now and then she would call to get advice. It was clear that while she appreciated the new technology, she wasn't terribly fascinated by it.

By this time, Grandpa Bobbie was no longer riding his bike because of the pain he was experiencing in his hip. He was also having trouble walking and standing for long periods. One Sunday afternoon, she and her family stopped by her parents'. It was supposed to be a short visit. Right away, Denise noticed an ankle wrap on her father's leg. "What's the matter with your leg, Dad?" she asked.

"Oh, I twisted my ankle getting off the elevator the other day."

"Does it hurt, Grandpa?" Rick asked, sounding concerned.

"Yeah, it's hurting a bit. That's the reason I decided to support it with this ankle wrap. I'm using my walker more often now, too."

"How long ago did this happen?" Denise pressed.

"About two days ago," her father responded.

"Grandpa, I think you should see a doctor," Ora chimed in.

"I agree," said Denise, "Don't take any chances; get it x-rayed, Dad."

With some hesitation, Grandpa Bobbie agreed that it might be a good idea. Just then the telephone rang and his wife picked it up.

"Hi Flo," she answered as she walked a few yards away from everyone. Flo was a friend of Grandma Rose and Grandpa Bobbie. The conversation was short. As Grandma Rose made her way back, she tapped the phone on her palm gently, turned to her husband and said, "That was Flo, and guess how she got to the dentist last Friday?"

"How?" asked her husband.

"She used the local senior center transportation service. Isn't that the service you mentioned to me a while back, Denise?"

"Yeah, that's one of them. How was it?" Denise asked with a hint of excitement.

"She said that it was actually better than she'd expected. She had to register with the center first and then she made a reservation for her trip. They sent a driver to pick her up and take her to the dentist.

"And they took her back home, too?" Grandpa Bobbie asked.

"Yes, she said that when she was finished, she called the transportation office and they sent a driver to pick her up and take her home."

Grandpa Bobbie nodded his head and said, "That's not a bad deal."

"That's great! Denise exclaimed. Did she mention if there were other passengers on board?"

"Yes, she said that there were two other people in the vehicle and she was the second person to be dropped off. She sounded satisfied with the service and the best part is—it's free!" They only accept donations."

Just then, Ora asked, "Would you like to give it a try, Grandpa?"

Her grandfather looked down at her eager face and smiled. Before he could respond, Denise interjected, "Dad, I think you should consider registering for the service. Right now you can't walk or stand for long periods and this sore ankle is going to add to your troubles. Besides, I'm not sure how much longer Mom will be able to drive. Both of you should sign up for the service."

Grandpa Bobbie looked back at Ora and said, "I think I'll give it a try, Baby!"

The good news is that once you are approved for the service, not only will you be able to use it for your medical appointments; you can use it to go to the senior center, grocery stores, and even for special trips that the center sponsors," Denise added.

Nodding her head, Grandma Rose admitted, "You know, Denise, the first time you brought up the issue of planning for other forms of transportation, I've been somewhat concerned. Now I feel relieved because at least I know that I have another means of travel when I have to give up my car keys. In fact, the rate at which things are going with me these days, I think that's going to happen very soon."

Denise looked over at her mother and smiled.

One month later, Grandpa Bobbie was getting on a senior center bus to go to the doctor. He had a smile on his face. Grandma Rose was next. Eventually, they both came to realize that while they may have to depend on others to meet their transportation needs, the change does not have to take away their independence and dignity. Soon they will be the ones calling a friend to talk about their "new ride."

Epilogue

In this modern society of ours there are two primary views on age and aging. Some people struggle against getting old and sometimes aging is even looked upon as a negative occurrence. It is sad to think that some older adults are made to feel useless, a burden to family and friends, and are remembered only on occasions such as birthdays or special holidays. Too often we hear of cases of abuse on the elderly by people responsible for their care. They endure substandard treatment such as physical, emotional, and sexual abuse, or financial exploitation in their own homes, in the homes of their relatives, or in long-term care institutions.

There is another view that age is beautiful and demands respect and honor. Many treat the elderly as individuals who are experienced, wise, and worthy of our praise and attention. This is the view to which I choose to subscribe. This is the mindset that I wish more of us would cultivate.

I believe that the older a person gets, the more he or she should be appreciated by others. An individual should be recognized and feel a sense of belonging. Age does not mean that a person no longer has any value. In fact, many are holding on to a treasure trove of information that can make a world of difference to many people. If we do not engage the elderly and tap into their intellect, their spirit, and take advantage of their willingness to share, we are doing ourselves and the next generation an injustice.

We should encourage our young people today to tap into the resources and talents of the elderly by associating and interacting with those they trust, starting with family members. This one-on-one, personal, unedited exchange can rival any information gained from the classroom, Internet, printed material, and other sources. Bear in mind that the elderly have already made their mark on life. Many have done well, and they feel a sense of accomplishment in knowing that their life was well spent in raising their children, making a positive impact on the world, and in training the next generation. Many are anxious to share their wisdom, relate their experiences, and offer advice on life as they see it. Let's not wait until they are no longer with us. We should take advantage of their wit and their ability to give guidance.

Whether it is a family member, friend, neighbor, we can each play a role in engaging the elderly in our community and encouraging them to seek opportunities for enrichment. Joining a senior center or taking advantage of similar programs provides a means of physical, emotional, and spiritual stimulation for those we love.

Bear in mind, the elderly may not move as quickly as they once did, so be patient and offer assistance when needed. The elderly may not speak as clearly as they used to, so be patient and listen keenly during conversations. The elderly may not hear as well as you do, so make eye contact, speak clearly and articulate your words—there is no need to shout. Be courteous and smile. We should make a conscious effort to develop the kind of patience and respect that will express to the elderly among us that they matter and we care. We should also accept the inevitability of aging and realize that in time, we will want patience, kindness, and respect to be reciprocated. Remember, older adults still have an opportunity to be productive members of our families, our communities, and our society if we accommodate them.

If you are nearing retirement age or are already retired, take deliberate steps to protect yourself and enrich your life. Discuss your legal, financial, and health matters only with people you trust. Don't isolate yourself; stay in touch with family members and old friends. Maintain a healthy diet, and an active and social lifestyle. Take advantage of the resources in your community—many of them are free and some of them you are already paying for.

Search for volunteer opportunities in your community and get involved.

Growing old is not a woe to humanity. It is everyone's right and privilege to grow old. We are all God's children. Live long! Live healthily and happily! Live with dignity!

Appendix A

State-Specific Agencies on Aging

Every state in the nation offers a full range of services to seniors. These services will vary from state to state. To find out the types of services that are available to you in your state, contact your state's office of the aging. Below is a directory of the offices of the aging for all 50 states and each organization's contact information. We hope you will find them useful.

ALABAMA
Department of Senior Services
770 Washington Ave.
RSA Plaza, Suite 470
Montgomery, AL 36130
334-242-5743, 1-800-243-5463
www.adss.alabama.gov

ALASKA
Commission on Aging
P.O. Box 110209

Juneau, AK 99811-0209
907-465-4879
www.alaskaaging.org

ARIZONA
Arizona Department of Economic Security
Division of Aging and Adult Services (DAAS)
1789 W. Jefferson Street (Site Code 950A)
Phoenix, AZ 85007
602-542-4446
https://www.azdes.gov/daas/aps/

ARKANSAS
Arkansas Department of Human Services
Division of Aging and Adult Services
P.O. Box 1437, Slot S-530
1417 Donaghey Plaza S.
Little Rock, AR 72203-1437
501-682-2441
http://www.daas.ar.gov/

CALIFORNIA
Department of Aging
1300 National Drive, Suite 200
Sacramento, CA 95834-1992
Phone: (916) 419-7500
TDD: (800) 735-2929
http://www.aging.ca.gov/

COLORADO
Division of Aging and Adult Services
Department of Human Services
1200 Federal Boulevard
Denver, CO 80204
Customer Service: (720) 944-3666
http://www.cdhs.state.co.us

CONNECTICUT
Division of Elderly, Community, and
Social Work Services
25 Sigourney St., 10th Floor
Hartford, CT 06106-5033
860-424-5274
1-866-218-6631
www.dss.state.ct.us/divs/eldsvc.htm

DELAWARE
Department of Health and Social Services
Division of Services for Aging and Adults with
   Physical Disabilities
1901 N. Dupont Hwy.
New Castle, DE 19720
302-255-9390
1-800-223-9074
www.dsaapd.com

DISTRICT OF COLUMBIA
Office on Aging

500 K Street, NE
Washington, DC 20002
202-724-5622
www.dcoa.dc.gov

FLORIDA
Department of Elder affairs
4040 Esplanade Way
Tallahassee, FL 32399-7000
850-414-2000
TDD: 850-414-2001
http://elderaffairs.state.fl.us

GEORGIA
Department of Human Resources
Division of Aging Services
Two Peachtree Street, NW, 33rd Floor
Atlanta, GA 30303-3142
404-657-5258
866-552-4464
http://aging.dhs.georgia.gov/

HAWAII
Executive Office on Aging
No. 1 Capitol District
250 S. Hotel Street
Suite 406
Honolulu, Hawaii 96813-2831
808-586-0100

http://hawaii.gov/health/eoa/index.html

IDAHO
Commission on Aging
341 W. Washington
Boise, ID 83720208-334-3833
www.idahoaging.com

ILLINOIS
Department on Aging
One Natural Resources Way, Suite 100
Springfield, IL 62701
217-785-3356
http://www.state.il.us/aging

INDIANA
Division of Aging and Adult Services
402 W. Washington Street, PO Box 7083, MS21
  Room W 454
Indianapolis, IN 46204
1-888-673-0002
www.in.gov/fssa/da

IOWA
Department on Aging, Elder Abuse Program
Iowa Department on Aging
Jessie M. Parker Building

510 E 12th Street, Suite 2
Des Moines, IA 50319-9025
515-725-3333
1-800-532-3213
http://www.aging.iowa.gov/

KANSAS
Department on Aging
New England Building
503 S. Kansas Ave.
Topeka, KS 66603-3404
785-296-4986
1-800-432-3535 (in Kansas only)
TTY 785-291-3167
http://www.kdads.ks.gov

KENTUCKY
Cabinet for Health and Family Services
Division of Aging Services
275 E. Main Street, 5C-D
Frankfurt, KY 40621
502-564-6930
http://chfs.ky.gov/dail/

LOUISIANA
Governor's Office of Elderly Affairs
P.O. Box 61
Baton Rouge, LA 70821-0061
225-342-7100

http://goea.louisiana.gov/
MAINE
Department of Human Services
Office of Elder Services
11 State House Station
32 Blossom Lane Augusta, Maine 04333
207-287-9200
1-800-262-2232
www.maine.gov/dhhs/oads/aging/

MARYLAND
Department of Aging
State Office Bldg., Rm. 1007
301 W. Preston Street
Baltimore, MD 21201-2374
410-767-1100
800-243-3425 (in state)
www.mdoa.state.md.us

MASSACHUSETTS
Executive Office of Elder Affairs
One Ashburton Place, 5th Floor
Boston, MA 02108
617-727-7750
800-882-2003 (MA only)
800-872-0166 (TTY)
http://www.mass.gov/elders/utility/elder-affairs

MICHIGAN

Office of Services to the Aging
P.O. Box 30676,
Lansing, MI 48909-8176
http://www.michigan.gov/miseniors

MINNESOTA
Board on Aging
Elmer L. Andersen Human Services Building
540 Cedar Street
St. Paul, MN 55155
651-431-2500
1-800-882-6262
TTY Service: 1-800-627-3529
http://www.mnaging.org/

MISSISSIPPI
Aging and Adult Services
750 North State Street
Jackson, MS 39202
(601) 359-49291-800-345-6347
http://www.mdhs.state.ms.us

MISSOURI
Department of Health and Senior Services
912 Wildwood
P.O. Box 570
Jefferson City, Missouri 65102
Phone: 573-751-6400
http://health.mo.gov
MONTANA

Senior and Long Term Care Division
Department of Public Health & Human Services
P.O. Box 4210
111 Sanders. Room 211
Helena, MT 59604-4210
406-444-5622
www.dphhs.mt.gov

NEBRASKA
State Unit on Aging
Department of Health & Human Services
P.O. Box 95026
301 Centennial Mall S.
Lincoln, NE 68509
402-471-3121
800-942-7830 (Nebraska only)
http://dhhs.ne.gov/Pages/aging.aspx

NEVADA
Division of Aging Services
Department of Human Resources
3416 Goni Road, Bldg. D-132
Carson City, NV 89706
775-687-4210
www.aging.state.nv.us

NEW HAMPSHIRE

Bureau of Elderly and Adult Services
State Office Park S.
129 Pleasant Street, Brown Bldg. #1
Concord, NH 03301
603-271-9203
1-800-351-1888
http://www.dhhs.nh.gov/dcbcs/beas/contact.
htm

NEW JERSEY
Division Aging and Community Services
Department of Health & Senior Services
P.O. Box 360
Trenton, NJ 08625-0360
877-222-3737
www.state.nj.us/health/senior

NEW MEXICO
Aging and Long-Term Services Department
2550 Cerrillos Road
Santa Fe, New Mexico 87505
505-476-4799
1-866-451-2901
www.nmaging.state.nm.us

NEW YORK
Office for the Aging
2 Empire State Plaza
Albany, NY 12223-1251
518-474-7012

http://www.aging.ny.gov

NORTH CAROLINA
Department of Health and Human Services
Aging and Adult Services
Taylor Hall
693 Palmer Drive
2101 Mail Service Center
Raleigh, NC 27699-2101
919-855-3400
http://www.ncdhhs.gov/aging

NORTH DAKOTA
Department of Human Services
Aging Services Division
1237 W Divide Ave, Suite 6
Bismarck ND 58501
Phone: 701.328.4601
TTY 1.800.366.6888
http://www.nd.gov/dhs/services/adultsaging

OHIO
Department of Aging
50 W. Broad Street, 9th Fl.
Columbus, OH 43215-5928
614-466-5500
1-800-266-4346

www.goldenbuckeye.com

OKLAHOMA
Aging Services Division
Department of Human Services
2401 N.W. 23rd St., Ste. 40
Oklahoma City, OK 73107
405-521-2281
1-800-211-2116
http://www.okdhs.org

OREGON
Seniors and People with Disabilities Division
500 Summer Street NE, E02
Salem, OR 97301-1073
503-945-5811
TTY 1-800-282-8096
http://cms.oregon.gov/dhs/spwpd

PENNSYLVANIA
Department of Aging
555 Walnut Street, 5th Fl.
Harrisburg, PA 17101-1919
717-783-1550
www.aging.state.pa.us

PUERTO RICO
Governor's Office for Elderly Affairs
1064 Ponce de Leon Ave.

P.O. Box 191170
San Juan, PR 00919
1-787-721-6121
http://www.agingcare.com/local/
  Puerto-Rico-Gobierno.PR

RHODE ISLAND
Department of Human Services
Division of Elderly Affairs
74 West Road
Hazard Bldg., 2nd Floor
Cranston, RI 02920
401-462-3000
TTY 401-462-0740
www.dea.state.ri.us

SOUTH CAROLINA
Lieutenant Governor's Office on Aging
1301 Gervais Street, Suite 350
Columbia, SC 29201
Phone: (803) 734-9900
1-800-868-9095
www.aging.sc.gov

SOUTH DAKOTA
Department of Social Services
Office of Adult Services and Aging
Richard E. Kneip Bldg
700 Governor's Drive
Pierre, SD 57501-2291

605-773-3656
1-866-854-5465
www.state.sd.us/social/asa

TENNESSEE
Commission on Aging and Disability
Andrew Jackson Bldg., Suite 825
500 Deaderick Street
Nashville, TN 37243-0860
615-741-2056
www.state.tn.us/comaging

TEXAS
Department of Aging and Disability Services
701 W. 51st Street
P.O. Box 149030
Austin, TX 78711-9030
512-438-3011
http://www.dads.state.tx.us/

UTAH
Division of Aging & Adult Services
195 North 1950 West
Salt Lake City, UT 84116
801-538-3910
1-877-424-4640
www.hsdaas.state.ut.us

VERMONT

Department of Disabilities, Aging and Indepen
dent Living
Division of Disability and Aging Services
103 South Main Street
Weeks Building
Waterbury, VT 05671-1601
802-871-3065
TTY 802-241-3557
http://dail.vermont.gov/

VIRGINIA
Department for the Aging and Rehabilitative
Services
Division for the Aging
1610 Forest Ave., Suite 100
Henrico, VA 23229
804-662-9333
1-800-552-3402
www.vda.virginia.gov/

WASHINGTON
Department of Social and Health Services
Aging & Disability Services Administration
P.O. Box 45130
Olympia, WA 985040-5130
360-725-2300
800-737-0617 (in-state)
www.aasa.dshs.wa.gov

WEST VIRGINIA
Bureau of Senior Services
190 Kanawha Blvd. E.
Holly Grove, Bldg. 10
Charleston, WV 25305
304-558-3317
877-987-3646
www.state.wv.us/seniorservices

WISCONSIN
Department of Health Services
Services for the Elderly
1 West Wilson Street
Madison, WI 53703-7851
608-266-1865
TTY 1-888-701-1251
http://www.dhs.wisconsin.gov/aging/

WYOMING
Department of Health
Aging Division
6101 Yellowstone Road
Cheyenne, WY 82002
307-777-7986
1-800-442-2766
http://www.wyomingaging.org

Appendix B

Resources for Seniors

Below is a list of organizations that provide relevant information on issues that affect the elderly.

AAA Foundation for Traffic Safety	800-305-7233	www.aaafoundation.org
AARP	888-687-2277	www.aarp.org
ABLEDATA	800-227-0216	www.abledata.com
Administration on Aging (AOA)	202-619-0724	www.aoa.gov/eldfam/eldfam.asp
American Alliance for Health, Physical Education, Recreation, and Dance	800-213-7193	www.aahperd.org
The American Heart Association	1-800-242-8721	www.americanheart.org
American Physical Therapy Association	800-999-2782	www.apta.org
American Society On Aging	415-974-9600	www.asaging.org
Arthritis Foundation	800-283-7800	www.arthritis.org
Disability Info.gov		www.disabilityinfo.gov

ELDERWEB	309-451-3319	www.elderweb.com
ExperienceWorks	866-397-9757	www.experi-enceworks.org
MealCall.org		www.mealcall.org
National Adult Day Services Association	800-558-5301	www.nadsa.org
National Association Of Area Agencies On Aging	202-872-0888	www.n4a.org
National Association Of State Units on Aging	202-898-2578	www.nasua.org
National Council On Aging	202-429-0787	www.nhcoa.org
National Institute On Aging	301-496-1752	www.nih.gov/nia
National Rehabilitation Information Center	800-346-2742	www.naric.com
National Resource Center on Supportive Housing and Home Modification	213-740-1364	www.homemods.org
National Safety Council	800-621-7619	www.nsc.org
National Senior Games Association	225-766-6800	www.nsga.com
Paralyzed Veterans of America	800-424-8200	www.pva.org
Points of Light Foundation	404-979-2900	www.point-soflight.org
President's Council on Physical Fitness and Sports	202-690-9000	www.fitness.gov
Senior Corps	800-424-8867	www.senior-corps.org

Service Corps of Retired Executives (SCORE)	800-634-0245	www.score.org
SeniorNet	571-203-7100	www.seniornet.org
Senior Job Bank	888-501-0804	www.seniorjob-bank.org
Senior Resource	877-793-7901	www.senior-resource.com
Senior Service America	301-578-8800	www.seniorser-viceamerica.org
Social Security Administration	800-772-1213	www.ssa.gov
Volunteers of America	800-899-0089	www.volunteer-sofamerica.org

Contact Information
Website: www.thompsonellisconsulting.com
Email: author@thompsonellisconsulting.com
Phone: 954-707-7907